Back to the Grindstone

Personal Recollections of the Sheffield Cutlery Industry

Herbert Housley

Back to the Grindstone

Personal Recollections of the Sheffield Cutlery Industry

Herbert Housley

The **Hallamshire** Press 1998

© 1998 The Hallamshire Press

The Hallamshire Press is an imprint of
Interleaf Productions Limited
Broom Hall, Sheffield S10 2DR

Typeset by Interleaf Productions Limited
Printed by The Cromwell Press, Trowbridge, Wiltshire.

British Library Cataloguing in Publication Data:
A catalogue record for this book is available from the British Library

ISBN 1 874718 28 8

Contents

Acknowledgements

My grateful thanks are expressed to the following people who have assisted me with this book:

Richard Caborn MP for reading the manuscript and writing the foreword, Keith Farnsworth and Pauline Shearstone for their invaluable support with the text and layout of the original book, *Grinders and Buffers*. Barry Nicholls, lecturer to the Abbeydale Writers Group of which I am a member, who first read and then corrected many of my mistakes. Sheffield Newspapers, The Sheffield City Library and Gerry Sweetman LRPS for permission to use some of their photographs. My mother and her sister Ellen, both now deceased, for their recollections of days gone by and for old family photographs. Sheffield Museums for allowing me to photograph and use the pictures of the Gas Engine at Kelham Island and the interior of the Manager's House at Abbeydale Industrial Hamlet. Pauline Climpson and her editor Pat Whitehead of *The Hallamshire Press*. Last but not least thanks to my wife Margaret who typed my original hand-written notes and who has helped me and supported me throughout and to the many others, too numerous to mention, who have helped me with this venture.

Foreword

Once again Herbert Housley has written a book which combines both a personal and historical account of Sheffield's cutlery trade.

Originally reluctant to enter the cutlery trade, Bert found himself apprenticed to his father at the age of fourteen, he was surprised by the pride the cutlery workers had for their job in what seemed such gloomy conditions. He was quick to pick up some of the skills of the cutlery workers but was forced to leave after being drafted for the armed forces at the age of eighteen.

Returning again to the trade, in 1947, and a boom time for Sheffield, he found his father's business had expanded and extended its workforce. After getting married in 1948 and then working for several firms in Sheffield he became equal partners, with his brother Barry, in his father's business.

Back to the Grindstone takes you on a journey into Sheffield's past through the eyes of a man who made an invaluable contribution to Sheffield's cutlery industry. This account is documented in a humorous and lively way by Bert who, fortunately, had the insight to note down the major events shaping his working life. He captures the spirit of Sheffield through the war years and after in this fascinating look at life.

Richard Caborn MP (Sheffield Central)
Minister for the Regions,
Regeneration and Planning, DETR
1998

Preface

The first part of this book, which has previously been published under the title *Grinders and Buffers*, contains reminiscences of my early life in the Upperthorpe district of Sheffield and my beginnings in the local cutlery trade. It tells of times long gone and of places which no longer exist. As such, it forms a kind of social history, telling of a way of life and of working practices which have disappeared. I dedicated the first book to the memory of those grand old craftsmen and women who were the salt of the earth, some of the finest people I have ever met—I was proud to have lived and worked amongst them.

Many people have told me how much they enjoyed *Grinders and Buffers*, so I decided to continue the story further. In *Back to the Grindstone* the original is still there but I have carried on from when I was called up, in 1943, to the mid 1950s. These are my personal recollections of life in the forces and of the first ten years of the post-war cutlery industry on my return to civilian life.

I dedicate this book to Tim, my Down's syndrome son who, but for his handicap, would have made a masterful cutler.

I shall donate all my royalties from this book to *Worthwhile Occupational & Recreational Krafts Limited* (WORK) a registered charity which I founded to provide meaningful employment, in a sheltered environment, for people with learning difficulties.

Herbert Housley
October 1998

Cutlery in the Blood

Born at number 24 Portland Street, in the Upperthorpe District of Sheffield, on Tuesday September 29th 1925, the second son of a self-employed knife grinder, I can well imagine that I arrived in the world with cutlery in my blood and the smell of the grinding wheel in my nostrils. No doubt my father, a typical representative of the traditional breed of Little Mesters, took time off to celebrate the birth of his second son though, like a lot of his pals in the Sheffield trades, he didn't need an excuse to have a drink. In those days the cutlery workers liked their pint of ale. Having arrived on Tuesday, I often wonder whether my father had spent the previous day in what was then the customary way; for they called it 'Saint' Monday in the local wheels. Little work was done on Mondays, and everybody gathered in the nearest pub to booze, play cards and have a sing-a-long. Few people went home quite sober, so perhaps Dad welcomed the chance to celebrate my arrival as a way of working off a hangover from the previous day!

Anyway, as the second son of Herbert and Annie Housley, I soon learned two things; first, we were poor—not as poverty-stricken as some of our neighbours but poor nevertheless, and second, we were the latest in a long line of cutlery folk. There's an old saying that where there's muck there's money, but if there was plenty of muck in the cutlery business there didn't seem to be much money about—not at our house anyway. I don't remember much about it really, but the first few years of my life coincided with a time of hardship and slack business in many of the local trades and, because there were many periods when there was little or no work for my father, the family finances were stretched to the very limit. Dad had to dodge his wheel and stone rents, and Mother had to take in washing to help make ends meet.

In those days I don't think there was much romance in work, and perhaps there wasn't much even at the best of times, for grinding wheels were dark, dingy and dirty places. Yet I think my father was a proud craftsman and took considerable pleasure in his skills. I also think he loved the fellowship and

Possing the Clothes on Washday. *The mangle, set-pot and the black-leaded stove were all features in the kitchen.*

good feeling that existed in the local trades, so that if there wasn't much money about there was no shortage of laughter and enjoyment amongst the cutlers, grinders and buffer lasses.

I was still in short trousers when I first recognised any sense of cutlery tradition in the family—not that anybody talked about it much or even suggested we were part of any kind of tradition—but everybody seemed in some way linked to cutlery and, I suppose, a lot of the talk that went on around me was about problems and conditions in the local trades. It was only years later, when I began to delve into the history of the family, that I discovered I was at least a seventh generation cutlery worker. On my father's side, his great-great grandfather, William Rushby, had been a knife grinder and publican at Little Matlock. That was in the 1840s, and he was probably far from being the first in that line. My father's grandfather, who lived in Jericho, off St Phillip's Road, Upperthorpe, was also a knife grinder but, for some reason I don't know about, his son, my paternal grandfather, went into file cutting.

This file cutter was Grandfather Housley, I remember him quite well. He was a typical Sheffield craftsman of his time: a man's man, independent, hard working and drinking. He and my grandmother lived in a poky two-roomed house in Hammond Street, and you can imagine the difficulties they faced

Charlie and Eliza Housley,
my Grandparents.

in raising twelve children in such a small place. It simply wasn't big enough to hold them all, in fact some of the children, all the lads, had to leave home every evening to sleep in a neighbour's house. The remarkable thing is that they took this total lack of privacy in their stride.

For all the financial stresses created in bringing up a dozen children, Grandfather Housley never lost his fondness for a pint of ale. It was always said of him that he could never walk past a public house without calling in. When money was really tight he often promised Grandmother he'd resist the

The wedding of the daughter of the landlord of the White Hart, *one of my grandfather's locals, in 1928. I was the page boy.*

Uncle John Housley, a typical Sheffield grinder.

This photograph, taken in 1914, shows some grinders and buffers employed by John Batts Ltd. First left back row shows Arthur Dunn and centre front row Ellen Dunn, my uncle and aunt.

lure of his local, but the smell of the beer as he passed the pub door invariably proved too great a temptation. He said one whiff of it weakened his resolve—Grandmother said it always meant he came home weak at the knees!

They called it a man's world then, the womenfolk no doubt had to suffer the consequences. However, few of the women lacked spirit, and Grandmother Housley certainly wasn't without quick wits and a sense of humour, as one incident I recall illustrates.

She had spent her last coppers on a small rabbit, and on this particular day there was just one helping of rabbit stew left. It had stood a long time in the oven awaiting the old man's return from the pub, and when he came in he was, as usual, slightly the worse for wear, and slumped into his armchair at the table. After Grandmother had set the plate of hot stew before him she popped next door to resume her gossip with a neighbour.

When she came back later she found the old man snoring, fast asleep and dead to the world but, to her horror, she saw the cat on the table just finishing off the stew. Poor Grandmother! She knew she couldn't produce another stew but then, looking at the remains of the gravy on the empty plate, she had a sudden brainwave. Dipping her fingers in the gravy, she turned and rubbed it on the edges of the old man's moustache.

Soon afterwards he awoke with a start and snapped 'Nah then, Liza, wot's for me dinner?'

'Tha's 'ad it, tha silly beggar. Look, there's gravy all o'er thi tash.'

He licked the edges of his moustache, smacked his lips at the cold taste of the gravy and agreed 'Ah, thar't reight, Liza, Ah can taste it!'

Two of my father's brothers, John and Joe, worked in knife grinding, and one of his sisters, Hettie, was a handle maker and another, Dolly, a file cutter. The cutlery tradition also extended into my mother's family. Mother was a Dunn, and her mother an Atkin, and both families went back several generations in pen and pocket knife making and other branches of the trade. Her brother Arthur was a knife grinder, another brother, Bill, a knife polisher, and Albert a razor grinder; her sister, Ellen, was a knife buffer for over 40 years.

The experience of my mother's family served to emphasise the hardships of the cutlery trade, especially in the inter-war years. Arthur, for example, endured long periods of unemployment during the depression of the Twenties and eventually elected to try his luck in Canada. On his first day in his new job in a Canadian grinding wheel he suffered a serious accident and died within a matter of hours. Bill stayed at home but spent long spells out of work and, when he finally got regular employment, he had the misfortune to suffer a heart attack and died at his workplace. Albert was more fortunate in that he survived the slump and during the war became a government inspector of cutlery and tools, eventually being rewarded with the MBE for his services.

Naturally, being surrounded by a family so closely involved in cutlery, I was soon familiar with the jargon and customs of the trades, and I wasn't very old, perhaps nine or ten, when I took over from my brother Charlie the task of delivering Dad's dinner to his workplace, so getting a closer look at life in a typical wheel.

Dad rented a wheel at the premises of R.F. Moseley, on Randall Street, just off Bramall Lane, and most lunchtimes I dashed home from school to collect his hot meal. This was contained in a white pudding basin covered with a plate, and the lot was wrapped in a giant-sized red-spotted handkerchief tied in a large knot at the top for easy handling and carrying. Catching a tramcar on Infirmary Road, I would travel to the foot of Ecclesall Road for a ha'penny fare and walk the short distance from there to Moseley's. Dad's dinner was still hot when I handed it to him and, surprisingly perhaps, I was always able to get back to Portland Street in time to eat my own dinner before returning to school.

If that was a fleeting introduction to the wheels of the central area, I suppose my education in cutlery was also developed by regular trips with Father when he was visiting the manufacturers' warehouses on Saturday mornings and during school holidays. Father always enjoyed these occasions, for it enabled him to keep up with trade gossip, and while he was collecting fresh blanks to take away for grinding and glazing, he was also delivering finished work—which meant that payment was due to him.

At the various warehouses, of course, I was always acknowledged then got to listen to some of the conversations about things like the quality of the work and the state of the trade. Soon I found myself intrigued by a grown-up world which seemed so far removed from school and the back streets of Upperthorpe. So, when I was about twelve, I was delighted when I managed to persuade my father to get me a little job at one of the firms for the duration of the school holidays.

One of Father's best customers was the firm of Maurice Stables & Co. Ltd., and Father was especially friendly with Mr Stables—he set me on as an errand boy. My duties involving fetching fish and chips, pork sandwiches, pies and peas, and cigarettes, from some of the small shops in Button Lane, and generally making myself useful. Of course, a casual errand lad is seldom fully occupied except at those periods when mealtimes are looming. As my father used to drop me off on his way to work and pick me up on his way home in the late afternoon, the days were long and I had a lot of time on my hands so, naturally perhaps, I spent much of it exploring and learning more about the mysteries of cutlery manufacture.

Stables & Co., who made low-priced high-volume cutlery, were based in Eldon Street, where they shared the premises with another cutlery firm, Brooksbank's, whose speciality was low-priced aluminium-handled knives.

The three-storey property, which was typical of a small cutlery works of the period, has long since disappeared, but I remember it vividly as it was then, some 62 years ago. A central archway led into a gloomy, cobblestoned yard onto which faced the windows of a string of small workshops. Stables' warehouse occupied part of the ground floor on one side, there was a cutlers' shop on the first floor, and the top floor housed mirror polishers.

Maurice Stables' wife, Sally, a rosy-cheeked, bonny lass with a ready smile and kindly eyes, was in charge of the warehouse, and the jolly banter and laughter that emanated from the womenfolk of that place made it a great attraction to a small and impressionable boy—but there were greater attractions. Being of a naturally inquisitive nature, I revelled in the opportunity that my temporary job afforded me of watching craftsmen from both Stables' and Brooksbank's working at their various tasks. I was forever asking questions or gazing silently as they performed the operations which so captured my imagination.

Seeing, for instance, the process of cutting out whittle-tang blades from sheet metal (rather like cutting out jam tarts from rolled out pastry) and watching the blades being heat-treated in readiness for hand grinding and glazing was a source of wonder to me. I discovered that, in the making of aluminium-handled knives, the ground and glazed blade was placed in a steel mould, shaped to form a handle and I watched in awe as the man dipped a ladle into the furnace pot containing molten aluminium and then poured it into the mould. The handles, I recall, were made in various shapes with many different decorations—the decorations being imparted by a pair of highly polished steel dies placed in a drop stamp. The drop stamp was, perhaps, the most fascinating object of my holiday adventuring. It was intriguing to see the operator stamping the handles with such precision and apparent nonchalance, holding them in position with his fingers barely an inch from the falling hammer or 'tup'. Those drop stamps, which operated like the French guillotine, were, of necessity, unguarded, and it looked a very dangerous operation to the small boy that I was then.

Ironically, whilst I was thinking of the threat of injury to the operator of the drop stamp, it never occurred to me that there might be unseen dangers lurking on the premises to threaten a mere errand boy. Then one day I happened to be making great haste to get my errands done, and, rushing down some greasy stairs too rapidly for my own good, I slipped and ended up with a broken wrist. The injury meant a sudden end to my first venture into the cutlery trade—I was sidelined for the rest of the holiday!

I can remember that I reflected that it had been a grand if brief experience. I spent a lot of time thinking of how much I had enjoyed gaining an insight into the various activities of an industry which had meant so much to my

A typical pre-war cutlery forge, in the foreground is a drop stamp, to the rear a spring-hammer.

family for many generations. However, even then, I regarded it all as a rather grim and unpleasant way to make a living, and I had my doubts as to whether I would want to follow in my father's footsteps—I didn't think I wanted to become a Little Mester. Fortunately, at the time, there was no need for me to make my feelings known at home and I could concentrate on enjoying being a schoolboy again—at least I could once I had recovered from my first industrial mishap!

Home

Home was a back-to-back house in a gas-lit, cobblestoned thoroughfare called Portland Street, which ran from Upperthorpe, at the top end, to just below Infirmary Road at the bottom. I remember my childhood there as a time of poverty and austerity but, all the same, we were happy and content. If we were oblivious of just how poor we sometimes were it was probably because Mother was such a wonderful manager. It was surprising what a housewife could achieve with a silver sixpence in those days, and I can never recall us ever going hungry or without the basic essentials of life.

By the standards of later generations, our house must seem very stark and basic, for it lacked many of the facilities and conveniences we now take for granted. The entire house had only three rooms: a living room which served also as a kitchen, my parents' bedroom on the first floor, and an attic in which brothers Charlie, Barry and I slept. There was also a small coal cellar, with an area at the top of the cellar steps (the cellar head) which had two shelves and served as a pantry. For most of my boyhood the living room and bedroom were lit by gaslight but, in the attic, we had to manage with the light provided by the gaslamp in the street outside. When electricity came, in about 1934, how bright that little old house seemed! It says much about the condition of the property that the entire street had been subject to a slum clearance order from before I was born, yet all the houses remained standing for another forty years!

Of course, the focal point of the house was the living room, and here the five of us passed most the waking hours we spent at home. It was, in turn, kitchen, dining room, washhouse, bathroom and parlour. There was only one source of water—the brass tap over the stone sink in the corner—and two sources of heat: the fire set in the Yorkshire range (complete with its oven and hob), and the grate beneath the set pot which was only brought into use on washdays. Mind you, considering that Mother used to take in

Interior of the Manager's House at Abbeydale Industrial Hamlet. Back-to-back houses, though smaller, had similar interiors.

washing to help supplement the family income, that set pot probably got more use than those in many other houses; and, of course, with lots of washing hanging on the indoor clothes line, especially in wintertime, our living room always seemed steamier and more crowded than most for much of the time!

Mother was not only a good manager of the pittance on which she had to bring up three boys and keep a husband fed and clothed, she was by nature one of life's toilers, never happier than when she was busy washing, cooking, baking, cleaning or sewing. That huge Yorkshire range which dominated one side of the living room was her pride and joy, and she devoted more attention and loving care on it than any grinder ever gave to his grindstone and tools. She blackleaded it every week until it shone like glass and you could see your face in it. On one side of the range there were some built-in cupboards extending from floor to ceiling, and on the other side stood the set pot and the dark brownstone sink. The sink, too, was constantly being subjected to Mother's elbow grease, for she insisted on a regular dose of rubbing-stone treatment which dried snow white and made it fairly sparkle.

The rubbing-stone was one of Mother's favourite household tools. She used it to scour the cellar steps, the front steps and the outside windowsill.

The stone she used was a piece from one of father's old grindstones. In those days there was an alternative to this, a donkey stone such as could be obtained from a rag-and-bone man in exchange for old clothes. Mother, however, always regarded donkey stone as inferior—much too common for a housewife with genuine pride in the results achieved by her work! She took as much pleasure in seeing that her doorstep was spotless as she did in ensuring that the net curtains at the window displayed a constant whiteness which indicated a clean and comfortable home within.

Washdays, of course, were always special occasions for Mother, a major operation in which she liked to be properly organised. She would light a fire beneath the set pot at the crack of dawn, fetch her tubs, dolly peg and washboard from the cellar, then, for a few hours, a sort of steamy, organised chaos would prevail as the living room was converted into a temporary laundry. Most of the time, she was able to hang out the washing in the communal back yard, but on rainy days it had to be hung on lines indoors—many's the time drying sheets and shirts inconveniently fell upon our heads just when we were sitting having a meal. As you can imagine, such incidents would provoke as much laughter as dismay, at least amongst the menfolk; but bath night was the time which produced the most regular doses of humour.

Once a week, the large zinc bathtub was brought up from the cellar and placed on the hearth at the front of the fire. A kettle would be constantly refilled with water and heated, then Charlie, myself and Barry, in that order, would take our turn in the tub. The source of much mirth was the fact that the tub had been repaired so many times it contained a score of soldered places, and these areas could prove rather painful and rough to the skin. Many times I scratched myself in tender places, especially my backside, during bathing sessions in that old tub! Thankfully, as time passed, we boys were able to seize the opportunity of using the facilities at the nearby public baths and, incidentally, once they had opened a public washhouse, too, that proved a boon to us all, but especially to Mother.

My parents slept in the bedroom above, which contained a double bed, wardrobe, dressing table and a marble-topped table which boasted a washbasin and jug—traditional fixtures in the upper rooms of most working class houses. We had a washbasin and jug in the attic, too, but I can never remember either set being used except when someone was ill. My parents' bedroom also had the luxury of a fireplace, but I can only once recall seeing it in use: a fire in any place other than the living room was considered the height of extravagance except in very unusual circumstances.

The attic, a room about twelve feet by ten, was, in a sense, the centrepiece of the boyhood world of we three Housley lads. We spent many hours lying awake at night, studying the patterns on the cracked and uneven ceiling, creating in our minds imaginary pictures and maps from the strange shapes formed by the plaster. It always amused us to lie there in the gloom, broken only by the reflected light of the gaslamp outside, making up stories and listening to the chatter and noise which drifted up from the Portland Arms pub across the road. On Saturday evenings, especially, we would be entertained by the singing of the pub's regulars, the sound always increasing in volume the nearer it got to closing time!

There were no such things, in our neighbourhood, as indoor toilets then, and if one of us had to answer the call of nature and didn't have the time or inclination to make the marathon trip downstairs to the outside toilets in the backyard, we had to use the white enamelled pot kept under the bed. It was always known as 'our Benjie's po' because it had once belonged to Mother's brother, Uncle Benjamin, who had lodged with our parents in the early days of their marriage. That pot was as much a source of pride in our attic as the family aspidistra was in the bedroom below. Today it survives only as a memory from a time when luxuries were few, whilst the aspidistra gave off cuttings which continue to remind us of those Portland Street days.

For some years Charlie, Barry and myself slept in an ancient four-poster double bed, the full history of which would probably make very interesting reading had it ever been recorded. However, as time passed, Charlie qualified for a single bed of his own. Two in a bed or three, I don't think it ever troubled us, for we always enjoyed the deep sleep of the young—until, that is, we were suddenly aroused by the siren which sounded at Basett's sweet factory every weekday morning at exactly five minutes to seven. It was the signal for hurrying footsteps in the street below, as men but mostly women rushed to clock in for a day's work, and whenever I think of early morning at Portland Street I remember how often I pulled myself out of sleepfulness to the echo of running clogs on the pavement outside. A second siren sounded at 7a.m. and any late-comers were locked out and had to answer to management.

The top of our street formed part of the junction of five roads which marked the start of the busy little shopping area of Upperthorpe. That junction was dominated by three buildings: the public library, the Upperthorpe Hotel, and Cartledge's pawnshop. I don't know about the influence of the library in those days, but I think the other two places served as a kind of barometer of the state of local trade and the condition of the district. There were times when the pub did the most business, but I fancy that more often than not the pawnshop had more patrons! However, despite the prevalence of poverty in the area, Upperthorpe was a happy place with an atmosphere of great friendliness and conviviality. Everybody was in the same boat and putting on a brave face and, in hard times, people seemed to rally round to help each other. Anyone who found themselves in difficulties could always depend on a neighbourly helping hand.

Mother, as I have said, was an excellent manager, but I can remember times when her purse was empty and she didn't, as the saying goes, have two ha'pennies to rub together. There was one person in the district, Mrs Foulstone, who was a bit like a mother to Annie Housley, and on those occasions when things got a bit desperate, even for Mother, she was often her saviour. Once, I recall, Mother didn't have a penny to her name and she reluctantly sent me to borrow sixpence from Mrs Foulstone. That dear woman unhesitatingly handed me a shiny silver tanner, and I knew it would enable Mother to produce a splendid meal—for as I've said, it was really remarkable how much a housewife could achieve with a sum that is only two-and-a-half pence in today's currency.

One thing was for sure, unlike Grandmother Housley, my mother never had to tell her husband that he'd eaten his rabbit stew when he hadn't! Mother would move heaven and earth to ensure that Dad didn't go hungry—and Dad never permitted himself to fall asleep when there was food on the table!

Upperthorpe Library, the focal point of the district. Outside the library political meetings were held and the Salvation Army held an open-air service every Sunday evening.

My Parents

Poverty was the name of the game in Portland Street, but if we lacked many of life's luxuries I don't think it prevented us from enjoying ourselves. As for me and my brothers, we didn't really think about our circumstances. We accepted the world as it was, and probably believed it was the same for everybody. Certainly we were never conscious of missing out on benefits which children in the more prosperous parts of the city might take for granted—there were no chips on our shoulders. My parents obviously knew that better conditions existed elsewhere but I don't think they ever envied anyone who happened to enjoy greater security. They were used to their own way of life, and they were happy enough.

They lived in Portland Street for over 40 years and I doubt if they ever seriously considered moving until they had to when their home was finally demolished. Mother might have suggested a move once or twice, but Dad wouldn't budge. Even when they did have to quit Portland Street, they only moved to another part of the district, to Bramwell Street, for I think they only felt comfortable in that part of Sheffield which was familiar—their 'own' part. In later years especially, I often felt that Dad could have helped make life easier for Mother, and a move might have improved the quality of their lives, but the truth was that they were essentially of their time and place, and perhaps they couldn't have changed even if they had wanted to.

Ironically, there were periods when we seemed better off than most of our neighbours, and there were other phases when we seemed to be worse off— at a disadvantage and denied the help others could get in really bad times. This was because my father's income often fluctuated from one extreme to another. When there was plenty of work, he could make a very reasonable living but, when there was no work in his trade, unlike so many of the other men in our street, he couldn't apply for Relief. There was no dole for the self-employed. I often think, looking back, that if he hadn't been so fond of his pint of beer and his flutter with the bookmakers, perhaps they could have

My parents, Herbert and Annie Housley, taken in the 1930s, these photos are the only ones I have of that period.

kept some cash in hand for those times when the workload dropped to next to nothing, but you couldn't change a man so firmly set in his ways.

One good thing about my father was that he was seldom defeated by circumstances. He was one of life's survivors, never stuck when it came to using his imagination and initiative if conditions demanded. As a knife-grinder, he was one of the best at what was a highly skilled and specialised job; and as a sub-contractor, or Little Mester, I fancy he was at the forefront among his rivals and colleagues. For instance, for as long as I can remember, he always had a motor car. This, remember, was in the days when very few working men owned a car. Indeed, most of his fellow Little Mesters were content to collect and deliver blanks in home-made wheelbarrows. Dad felt it would be quicker and more economical to use a car. Possession of a car, of course, put the Housleys in a class of their own in Portland Street, and the vehicle was a source of considerable attraction as it stood in the road outside our house. Little wonder, then, that some of our neighbours thought we were better off than we were! The car was like a magnet to other little kids in the street who would come and play on and around it for hours. Dad garaged it up the road in Upperthorpe, and almost every time he went out to put it away he would find as many as twenty children waiting to beg a short ride, he usually said 'Jump in' and as many as it would hold did so.

Dad used to pay about £5 for a second-hand car—perhaps a bull-nosed Morris or an old Chevrolet—which he'd run for about six months. Then he'd sell it for fifty shillings and raise the rest to buy a replacement. Thus we had a succession of vehicles of all shapes and sizes, and the fact that we had another 'new' car would flash along the street and bring scores of young admirers to view it.

When times were especially bad, Dad's old car invariably proved its value. To generate a bit of essential income, he would use it to run fishing parties to Boston, or other parts of Lincolnshire, with several enthusiasts packed inside and baskets tied all over the outside. Or, he would hire himself and the vehicle out for weddings. For these occasions Mother had made white covers for the seats and ribbons for the bonnet, and she would ensure that Dad's best suit was neatly pressed. My brothers and I would spend all the eve of the wedding washing and polishing the car until it shone almost as bright as mother's Yorkshire range. So, Dad was never stuck when money was tight—though sometimes he'd prefer to put his faith in winning a few bob in a local tossing ring (for he was fond of pitch and toss). On other occasions the poacher would turn gamekeeper, in the sense that he would set himself up as a temporary bookmaker, in the firm belief that the bookie always fares better than the punter in the long run!

If Dad felt secure in his little house in Portland Street, and always declined to consider moving elsewhere, it wasn't because he spent a lot of time at home. On the contrary, his favourite abode when not at the wheel was the pub, and if he was a man of a few words in our house he always seemed to have plenty to say when he was enjoying a pint with his cronies. In his book, there was always ample time to stumble home to supper and bed when the pub closed its doors!

My father was a tall, slim chap but, naturally, he had a large beer belly, he was one of that old breed of typical Sheffield workmen who no longer exist. He worked hard, played hard, and always believed in what he called 'the Old Act'—which meant that he could go his own way but his woman's place was in the home. He left the bringing up of his three sons entirely to Mother, seldom interfering. Mother, for her part, simply accepted her lot, and though Dad's code permitted her to join him at the pub for the last half-hour on a Saturday evening, she seldom did so. She was quite content to stay at home, for she wasn't fond of beer—one glass could put her 'off-colour' for days.

It might seem that Dad was a selfish old devil, but I don't think he was consciously so. He was, as I've said, a man of his time and place, and in those days the menfolk simply didn't consider anyone else, they went about their daily lives almost as if nobody else existed. Somehow it never occurred to them that there were times when it was necessary to view matters from another's point of view—especially in their own families. Yet, if Dad invariably lived exactly as he wanted, he was not a bad father. I can never remember him hitting us as children, and when he had money he was always generous. If, in retrospect, he seems to have been in some ways a less than ideal husband, he was never selfish in a monetary sense. He'd give his last ha'penny away to a colleague or, indeed, to us; and though it was no doubt largely due more to Mother's good management than Dad's consideration, we never went short of the essentials. I fancy that if it had ever come to a stark choice between buying a pint and paying for a meal for his children, we would have got our food.

Mother carried him about and, being his willing servant, I think she enjoyed it in that uncomplaining way that was so common amongst women then. If we boys thought that Dad gave her a hard life, I think Mother considered it heavenly compared with what she had known before she married him. Perhaps she felt that she owed him everything because he had rescued her from a troubled and meaningless life. Anyhow, she thrived on a marriage which, with the hindsight of more than sixty years, may seem to have lacked many of the good things we nowadays take for granted, but yet was basically sound and happy.

Born in Copper Street, off Shalesmoor, Mother was one of about eight children, six of whom survived childhood. Her father, a labourer at the Neepsend Gas Works was, by all accounts, a pleasant, easy-going chap whose great passion was playing the melodeon. His wife, my grandmother, was very houseproud and liked to have everything spick and span, and the family lived in comfort and cleanliness even if they never had much money.

Unfortunately, Grandmother Dunn died suddenly of typhoid at the age of 30, and Mother's father remarried—the new Mrs Dunn proving very different from her predecessor. I think that Mother (who was then about nine years old) and the others had a torrid time in the much-changed circumstances. As they soon had no fewer than five stepbrothers and stepsisters, no doubt the young Dunns felt somewhat neglected; perhaps it was no surprise when, at the age of 14, Mother escaped by going into domestic service.

I don't know the circumstances under which Mother met Dad, but she was about 20 years old when they married at St Stephen's Church. I do, however, know two things about the wedding. For a start, Dad reversed the traditional pattern, in that it was the bridegroom who arrived late at the altar—no doubt he'd spent his final hours of freedom in a pub! Secondly, that they probably married ahead of schedule, for at the time Mother was already expecting my brother Charlie. Of course, in those days such a situation was far from uncommon, and though it may have caused a few raised eyebrows in some parts of the family, it certainly didn't prevent my parents from enjoying the occasion—my father's family never missed an opportunity for a knees-up!

Dad, born at Jericho, off St Philip's Road, was already working for himself. Having started work at 14 in a grinding wheel, he had quickly shown himself a young man with flair and ability. It is well known that in the grinding trades of Sheffield the step from working as an employee to being self-employed was but a short one, and Dad was his own master by the time he was 18. In taking this step he was following the traditional path but, as there were some who preferred to let others take the initiative, at least it shows that, from the beginning, Dad was very much his own man, confident of his abilities and sufficiently independent and determined to make his own way.

I know he rented a workplace at Petty's Wheel, later moved to another wheel in Boston Street, and had a spell at the famous old Kelham Island Wheel; but by the time I was old enough to recognise what he was doing, he was renting five grinding troughs (pronounced trow) at R.F. Moseley's place in Randall Street and employed about ten people. Moseley's, of course, had their own workforce and rented workshops to other local craftsmen. This old firm no longer exists, but the name survives in local history books because old Moseley was the first man to recognise the significance of Harry Brearley's discovery of stainless steel, his firm having the distinction of being the first manufacturers to use the material in the production of cutlery.

R.F. Mosley's yard, Randall Street, as it is today.

There is no doubt that, in his time, Dad must have had his share of ups and downs as a knife grinder, for in the span of his career the local trades experienced some sharp fluctuations in fortunes. He certainly knew all about the cycles of boom and slump and he witnessed a lot of changes. When Dad started work, for instance, they were still using natural grindstones made from local sandstone, these were not only more dangerous than the artificial stones, which were introduced in about 1920, but were ten times more unhealthy. They used to fill the workshops with dust and dirt and many a grinder contracted silicosis and other lung diseases which led to premature death. Perhaps the advent of the artificial stone lengthened Dad's life, anyway, he lived to be 78 and I cannot remember him having any of the health problems suffered by some of his early contemporaries, he always made sure the dust was well washed down with beer.

Dad's biggest problem, I think, was keeping up with his dues and demands. In good times and bad, he had to pay his wheel rent, his stone money, and wages to the people he employed. Only then could he calculate his own income. When trade was slack I can well believe that he suffered a few nightmares. His rent for the premises was based on the number of troughs he hired, the figure including the cost of the power which ran the grindstones and other equipment, he also had to make a weekly payment on each of the grindstones, too. In those days a Little Mester seldom bought a grindstone outright, they cost between £80 and £90 each, and so to purchase five would cost well over £400—an astronomical sum then. So the grindstones were acquired on the never-never, and as the grindstones lasted only about 10 months this hire purchase payment was as constant as the rent. It is true that when the six-foot diameter stones had been worn down, they could be sold to pen- and pocket-knife grinders (who in turn subsequently sold them to razor grinders); but a couple of accidents and few broken stones would soon increase the pressure on a man's finances. So perhaps it was no surprise that there were occasions when Dad would be absent when the rent man or the stone man called!

Apart from the occasional crisis—one or two of which must have been pretty serious when a bad spell continued for months—I think Dad always managed to make ends meet one way or another. After all, he was a man with a knack of surviving, and the fact that he lived to such a good age clearly indicates that he was made of stern stuff. Indeed, I would suggest that the toughest phase of his entire life was perhaps his final years for, unfortunately, at the age of 74, in the early 1970s, he got gangrene in a toe and had to have a leg amputated. For a man who had always been so active and independent, you can imagine what a terrible blow it must have been to suddenly find himself confined to a wheelchair and totally dependent on others. Yet it was typical of him that as he recovered in hospital, his chief concern was how his handicap might affect his social life.

'What am I going to do?' he asked me. I told him that he would still be able to go to the pub, talk to his cronies, have a drink, play cards and dominoes, and have a bet on the horses. On the very first day he went home, we made certain he was taken to his local pub, The Boomerang, and so long as someone was able to wheel him there he was happy. It helped that they were subsequently re-housed in a flat for the disabled, just off St Philip's Road.

Of course, the circumstances didn't make life any easier for Mother but, in the event, perhaps it was one of the most settled periods in her marriage. At least she knew where Dad was—holding court in The Boomerang—and she was quite content to continue lavishing her attention on the man who had always been the pivot on which her life revolved.

The death of my brother, Charlie, while a Japanese prisoner during the war, was the most cruel and painful blow to Mother, but it was never the debilitating experience she suffered when Dad died in January 1977, four years after the loss of his leg. She had been so involved, for so long, in catering for his every whim, indeed literally carrying him about, that her life suddenly seemed empty and meaningless. For two or three years she simply did not know what to do with herself, and it took her a long time to adjust to widowhood.

Mother died, at the age of 89 in 1988, and she probably enjoyed more comfort and ease in her later years than she ever imagined possible in her early life. Like many old people, she seemed to have shrunk with the passage of time, but in her prime she was a big, strong woman. She has often told me that she more or less brought up her brothers and sisters, and recalls that she used to fight to protect her younger bothers William, Albert and Benjamin—and sister Ellen. I can well imagine that she lacked little physical courage, and if she placed herself at the beck and call of Dad it wasn't because she was in any way scared of him. On the contrary, many is the time I have seen her put him in his place. In her heyday she had quite a fiery temper, and I recall that when Dad came home drunk they had many a battle. They didn't argue a lot, really, and there was never any kind of running feud in our house, but when the occasion demanded it they could trade verbal blows with remarkable vigour.

On one occasion I especially remember, she was busy ironing when Dad walked in, more drunk than sober, and they soon got to arguing. He must have said something which caused Mother's patience to break, for she threw the hot flat-iron at him! Fortunately she missed the target, but I can well imagine that, had the iron hit him, she would have been the first person to rush to Dad's aid for there is no doubt that she loved him, despite all his faults.

My parents Golden Wedding in 1970. It was held at the Boomerang *in Fawcett Street, not a stone's throw from where they lived.*

When I
was a Lad

I **think some famous poet once said** that heaven lies about us in our
childhood. Well, I don't think there was anything heavenly about
Upperthorpe in my early years, but I suppose it is fair to say that, with the
eyes of a boy, I looked upon it as a bright and happy place and, for the most
part, I imagine I was blind to the poverty and struggle, seeing shades of gold
amid those cobblestoned streets and black-grey buildings.

I cannot ever recall being bored as a boy. We were never short of
something to do and most of the amusements and entertainment came
entirely free of charge: from playing at 'Hopping Tommy' in the playground
at Upperthorpe School, to having a game of football either on the tip at
Crookesmoor or nearer home in Oliver's Straw Yard (and in both pastimes,
it helped if one was skilled at the shoulder charge!) Even before I was old
enough to go to school, I had discovered the delights of the local baths.
Possession of a scholar's ticket enabled me to get in for a penny but I soon
learned that anyone showing any ability at swimming could qualify for a free
pass; so I quickly staked my claim—and there were times when I passed the
whole day in those baths!

The Tabernacle Congregational Church in Portland Street was the focal
point of social life in the area, there was always something going on there in
those days of high unemployment and severe austerity. For boys, there was
the Cubs or the Scouts and for boys and girls, the Band of Hope, Young
Britons and games facilities. Even the school 'bobby', old 'Pop' Jones, was
someone we enjoyed coming face-to-face with at the Tabernacle, for, being
a Welshman, he ran the choir; and there was nothing quite like a good
hymn-singing session under his direction. The Vicar's wife and his daughter
invariably arranged a succession of little shows and entertainments, and these
events were always supported with great enthusiasm by folk who couldn't
afford to go into the city centre to see the professionals perform at the
Empire or Lyceum.

The Vicar, the Reverend Sidney Tredinnick, was a wonderful chap who put his heart and soul into caring for his flock, many of whom often referred to him as 'the poor man's lawyer' for, if anyone had problems or was in trouble, he was always there to offer help and advice, he had a rare flair for sorting things out quickly and painlessly. One thing about him that was unusual for the time was that he liked to visit the pub, always enjoying a glass of beer and the company of the regulars. He was often seen carrying a jugful of ale back to the vicarage afterwards.

Whitsuntide was always one of the Vicar's favourite celebrations, he delighted in seeing all the children in their bright new clothes: the girls in white dresses, the boys in suits. He would lead us all in hymns at the morning service and then off we would march round the corner to sing to the patients in the grounds of the Royal Infirmary. After that, the Vicar would stride out proudly as we children climbed the hill to join the traditional Whit Sings in Weston Park.

The Housley boys weren't especially religious, but we enjoyed the hymns and the stirring music of the church, and most Sundays we would get a double dose. In the morning the Salvation Army would march up Portland Street enroute from their Infirmary Road headquarters to the hospital grounds, and it was always rather thrilling to see their banners flying and hear the band playing. Later in the

Class 1 Upperthorpe Infants School 1930. I am standing far right, back row.

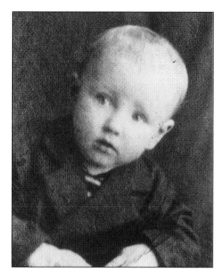

My younger brother, Barry, in 1932.   *A school photo of me taken in 1931.*

day they would return to hold an open-air meeting in the square outside Upperthorpe Library.

Money, of course, was a scarce commodity in the district, especially amongst the children. My brothers and I would always look forward to collecting a weekly penny from Grandmother Housley and sometimes we would also manage a penny or a ha'penny from Grandfather Dunn. When ready cash was not forthcoming from parents or relatives, we'd often go off in search of some empty jam jars as four of these would earn us a penny from old Collins, the rag-and-bone man, whose place was at the bottom of our street. Mother might not have been fond of the ragman's donkey-stone, but we were more than happy to accept a few pennies from him! After all, a penny would buy a quarter-pound of sweets, and a ha'penny gain us admission to the pit for the Saturday morning children's show at the Roscoe cinema. If we were able to afford it, and providing the film was one we really wanted to see, we would splash out a whole penny on a visit to the Oxford cinema—being just up the road, it was more convenient!

For most of the time, however, we didn't have two ha'pennies to rub together, so we would settle for a healthy walk which cost nothing at all. In those days we used to go walking regularly, tramping miles just for the pleasure of it. Strange to think that walking was such an adventure, but it was, and along the way there was always something to capture the attention of an imaginative and inquisitive boy. Sometimes the Sunday School teacher, Mr Gray, would lead us on our walks, but more often we took off on our own—to Weston Park, the Bole Hills, or Rivelin. Rivelin was a favourite spot, there we would strip naked and swim in the river, (this being in the days before the paddling pool was built). Sometimes, if we had a few coppers between us, we would take a tramcar to the Moorfoot, then walk as far as Millhouses Park. The big attraction there was the outdoor swimming pool. Unfortunately, we seldom possessed the price of admission, but, being lads without any fear of the consequences if we were caught, we got in by climbing over the fence. One special source of amusement within those walls was that area reserved for nude sunbathing—we were fascinated by the sight of grown men lying about without a stitch of clothing on!

Naturally, as boys will, we got into our share of scrapes—and we didn't have to go far from home to do that. Portland Street then contained a range of shops, from a butcher's to a pawnbroker's, but the big attraction was the sweet factory, famous as the home of Bassett's liquorice allsorts, which drew us like a magnet.

The roof of the factory, which could be reached over the back of the Tabernacle Church, contained skylights to brighten the premises below. We soon discovered that by tying our orange ropes (the stuff used for tying up orange boxes, and therefore freely available from the greengrocer's) to the roof trusses, we could lower ourselves through the skylight into the treasure house of goodies below. Of course, it was seldom that we reached and returned from our goal without alerting the timekeeper-cum-caretaker, Mr Beckett, he was usually quick to give chase to the young intruders. Once when he caught me I received a hearty thrashing. I suppose I deserved it, for what we were doing was stealing, really, but at the time we didn't think of it as such. It was just a great adventure.

For all the counter-attractions of life outside of school, I proved to be a fairly successful pupil. At least, I did well at my lessons and when I took the 11+ examination in 1936, I passed with flying colours. Strange as it may seem, I filled in the forms myself when they were sent from the Education Department for us to nominate a choice of school. As it happened, I qualified for my first choice and went to Carfield Intermediate School; it was a source of much amusement to me in later years that my second choice had been the illustrious King Edward VII Grammar School—I was clever enough to get to my first choice, but not my second! I enjoyed my time at Carfield, distant though it was from Upperthorpe, but I suppose I was happy enough to leave when my schooling ended prematurely owing to the outbreak of war in 1939. When we broke up for the summer holidays of July of that year, however, I didn't know that I would not return.

I remember that summer holiday in 1939 very well, for, in the midst of all the typical adventures which occupy a boy heading for his fourteenth birthday, I had an accident. Ironically, it happened not whilst climbing on rooftops but when I was combing my hair in the house! Mother happened to be doing the cleaning at the time, and had lifted the heavy brass fender onto its end, I was gazing into the mirror above the fireplace (no doubt thinking how handsome I looked) when the fender suddenly slipped and crashed onto my foot.

At the hospital I learned that I had broken my big toe, but all my lower leg was put into plaster. The nurse said I must remain at the Infirmary until the plaster had set properly, but as I was impatient to get home I told her that I had transport waiting outside. This 'transport' was in the form of a home-made trolley made of an old orange box and four old pram wheels. As it had enabled my pals to get me to the casualty department, surely it would get me safely home again. Unfortunately, as I climbed into the trolley I inadvertently put my full weight on the damaged foot and my pot cracked. So, when I returned to hospital the following day, the nurse frowned and said the plaster would have to be removed and reset—and this time she made me wait there until it had solidified!

I was still limping about on that pot when, following the outbreak of war, I learned that normal schooling was not being resumed on schedule. Along with my colleagues, I was instructed to collect my text and exercise books from Carfield, and was told that groups of pupils in various districts could expect to receive instructions and be set work by a visiting teacher who would call at chosen homes once a week. However, as I was about the only pupil from Carfield living in Upperthorpe, the weeks passed and I got no visit from my teacher. I was, in any event, in my final term and, in truth, somewhat frustrated to think that though I had my birthday in September I had to remain a schoolboy until Christmas. The added frustration of waiting for a teacher who never came soon wore out my patience so, after a while, it didn't take much effort on my part to persuade my parents to file the application which would enable me to end my schooling as soon as I reached my fourteenth birthday.

Dad was quite happy to take the action that would enable me to start work in the autumn, but it dashed his hopes when I revealed that I didn't want to go into cutlery. Life in a grinding wheel was dirty, noisy, wet and miserable, and it wasn't for me. So, politely but firmly, I declined to join the old man at Randall Street. To my surprise, and relief, Dad accepted my decision with little more than a shrug of the shoulders. Of course, he was disappointed, especially as my older brother, Charlie, had also failed to follow in his footsteps, and I'm sure he had been banking on me.

In truth, Charlie's experience perhaps made it easier for me to say no. You see, a few years earlier Dad had persuaded Charlie to go into the grinding

Beside my brother's grave,
Chungkai 1985.

Gunner Charles Housley, who died
whilst a Japanese P.O.W.

The bridge across the River Kwai that Charles helped to build.

General view of Chungkai War Cemetery where thousands of soldiers, who died building the railway, are buried.

wheel when he left school, but it had proved a mistake. Charlie disliked it so much and was so unhappy that it led to a great deal of friction at home. The situation built up into one of those typical battles of wills that occur sometimes in most families; but in the end Charlie had been allowed to quit the wheel and go his own way. No doubt Mother had a hand in the affair, for, as I have indicated, there were times when her opinion carried more weight than Dad liked to admit.

In referring to Charlie, I often wonder about the way fate dealt with him. He eventually became a moulder at the English Steel Corporation and, being in a reserved occupation, found himself exempt from the call-up when the war began. However, it wasn't long before he volunteered and went off to join the Royal Artillery and was posted to the Far East. We never saw him again. Via Singapore he went to Malaya where he was captured by the Japanese and put to work on the notorious Burma Railway. He contracted cholera there, and after his death was buried in the Chungkai War Cemetery in Thailand, just downstream from the famous bridge on the River Kwai. Many years later I took my family to visit his grave and, as I stood in that now beautiful and peaceful setting, I asked myself if Charlie would have survived had he stayed in cutlery and been called up in the normal way in 1939. Surely then the pattern of his army career would have taken an entirely different course.

Charlie's death was, of course, still in the future as I dressed in overalls for the first time in that autumn of 1939, having got myself a job in the Corporation Street works of Mellowes Limited, where, operating a drilling machine, I was the boy assistant to a window-frame assembler called Sonny Fletcher.

Dear old Sonny, what an experience it was for a new youngster like me to work alongside him. What an introduction to the grown up world! He was the first gay person (or at least I think he was, I never really found out) I ever met, and I'll never forget how astonished I was to discover that he wore make-up. He spoke in a light, effeminate voice and was a man of gestures, I have to admit that his manner rather puzzled me at first, yet he was harmless and, indeed, I enjoyed the time I spent working with him. Not only did he teach me the job, but he kept me entertained and amused—there were times when it was worth my 12s 6d wages just to listen to him. Of course, he was well known in Sheffield, he was a popular club comedian and local master of ceremonies. He used to MC the dances at the Cutlers' Hall—a place which in those days I associated solely with dancing and never thought of as having anything to do with the cutlery trade!

Unfortunately, my association with Mellowes came to a sudden and unexpected end after only a few months. The government decided that in the wartime conditions prevailing, window assembly was non-essential production. Thus, overnight, the firm shut down the operation and gave that part of their workforce notice to quit.

Now it was my turn to suffer disappointment and Dad's to feel that the Fates had helped his cause. 'Right!' he announced, 'You're coming to work for me' and I found myself back at Moseley's Wheel, not delivering Dad's dinner but working as an apprentice table-knife grinder. I was destined to discover quite a lot about cutlery and meet many amusing and delightful characters during the next four years.

At the Wheel

At the time I started out as an apprentice table-knife grinder at Moseley's Wheel, Sheffield was still the cutlery capital of the world, and though the workshops in which cutlery was made may have been anything but bright or pleasant places, the local craftsmen were proud of their reputation as highly skilled makers of top quality products which were the best of their kind.

The premises in which I worked, although they had obviously seen considerable changes, remained typical of the sort of place in which grinding and other skills had been practised for at least six or seven generations. True, the grinders had progressed from water power to steam and finally to gas, but the basic methods of operation and the philosophy and customs were largely unchanged. The natural grindstones had been replaced by man-made non-silicon stones which were less lethal, and the notorious practice of rattening, the removal or destruction of tools and other appliances to enforce payments or fines to the unions, had become a thing of the very distant past. In many respects, however, conditions were little improved, and the grinder still worked amidst a mixture of dirt, damp, darkness and danger. The people themselves retained most of the traditional traits of their trade; a fierce independence, a passion for a pint of ale and a sense of being, somehow, members of a unique breed. I didn't know it then, but I had become part of an industry which was not only different and special but, sadly, one which was destined to all but disappear within the span of my own working life.

In those days Sheffield boasted hundreds of cutlery and silverware manufacturers ranging from firms who employed a handful to others whose workforce might total seven hundred. These included many large companies whose names were household words and in whose premises every process in the manufacture of a wide range of cutlery could be completed, all done by their own employees. On the other hand, there were firms who were also famous names, yet they did not employ any direct labour at all, choosing

A gas engine now in operation at Kelham Island Industrial Museum.

A typical grinding wheel.

instead to have all their products made by an army of skilled outworkers who specialised in a single process. Thus an order for a batch of knives, for instance, could pass from one independent craftsman to another, from grinding wheel to cutlers' workshop, as the transformation from blank to finished product took place.

Sheffield had hundreds of self-employed and highly-skilled sub-contractors who rented small workshops and were call Little Mesters or Missis Buffers—grinders, hand forgers, smithers, die sinkers, toolmakers, polishers, hafters, cutlers, spoon and fork buffers, spoon and fork filers, hardeners, silversmiths, hollow-ware buffers, engravers, etchers, and so on. It had long been traditional for people to set themselves up and work on their own, in a rented workshop, and many of these Little Mesters made use of fellow craftsmen who sought the independence of self-employment but did not wish, or could not afford, to rent separate premises. The latter liked to work virtually as they chose, at a pace that suited them, and to be paid according to what they produced without taking the ultimate responsibility. Thus the Little Mester and his team ensured that almost every process in the industry could be, and was, done on an outworker or subcontractor basis. It seems almost unbelievable that this, once huge, network of independent craftsmen and women has gradually disappeared until all those once-traditional figures of Sheffield's cutlery industry have almost ceased to exist.

Moseley's premises alone gave work to about 200 people, with about half of them in that firm's employment and the rest independent craftsmen renting the remaining small workshops. Dad rented five troughs in a ground-floor wheel and had nine or ten people working for him. On the floor above was another grinding wheel of exactly the same proportions and the third-storey workshops were occupied by several cutlers and a scissors manufacturer. Elsewhere in the wheel there were other places used by polishers, buffers and cutlers.

As a boy, delivering dinners to Randall Street, I had always described father's workplace as 'like the Black Hole of Calcutta' and I didn't change my opinion when I finally and reluctantly went back there to begin my apprenticeship. Indeed, it seemed to me darker and more unpleasant than ever, for there was no ventilation and the only illumination was the electric lighting. Because of the war, all the outside walls and windows had been completely covered by scores of heavy sandbags—natural light and the flow of fresh air were completely excluded. Dad explained that the sandbags were intended to offer extra protection to the property in the event of a visit from the German bombers. In fact, our workshop had been converted into an emergency air-raid shelter—which explained why an array of steel girders had been fitted to reinforce the ceiling. I felt I was trapped within the airless walls of a prison, and it was enough to give a lad nightmares. Just to add to my dismay, I learned that our workshop was a favourite abode of rats and mice—attracted by the mutton suet used to lubricate the axle bearings of the grindstones and in the preparation of the glazers for buffing.

By the time of my introduction to the cutlery industry, of course, the days of water power had long since passed, my only link with it was that Uncle John had personal experience and knowledge of the system. Steam power, too, had gone, though evidence of this era still existed at Moseley's. The original engine-house survived, as did its adjoining 100-foot chimney— though in my time, because of the fear of air raids, I was to see about 60 feet lopped off the chimney for safety reasons. The once all-powerful steam engine had disappeared, but I heard tales of its prowess and was told that it had been so big that it had done the work which now required three gas

R.F. Mosley's chimney, 60 foot was removed in 1940.

engines. It was explained to me that gas engines were more efficient, as they didn't require an army of men to fuel them with coal; and gas could be turned on and off at the touch of a switch.

So my attention was focused on the gas engines, and brought me into contact with Harry Marriott, one of the many great characters who came into my life at the wheel. It didn't take me long to appreciate that Harry was totally devoted to those engines, giving them all the affection, attention and loving care that a hen might give her chickens. Harry lived on the premises and was both wheel caretaker and general mechanic, responsible for the maintenance of all the machinery on the premises. Then about 50 years old, he had followed his father into the job, he was plainly an intriguing and knowledgeable chap but he was not the type to encourage the attentions of an inquisitive lad. There was about his manner a sternness which precluded all small-talk, and it always seemed to me that he was perpetually preoccupied with his beloved gas engines. Wearing a cap to cover his hairless head, he was frequently to be seen dashing to or from one of the engine houses, sometimes still wearing his carpet slippers and, perhaps, eating—for, being a man constantly on the move, he seldom had the chance to finish a meal in peace.

There were two large engines, one of which served the 40 or so people occupying our part of the wheel. Then there was a smaller engine, it could be described as the baby of the trio for it certainly demanded more nursing than its bigger brother. Poor old Harry and his assistant, Ernest Wright, were constantly in attendance. Never can there have been a more temperamental engine and I doubt if there was ever a man who fussed over one like Harry.

Harry was a genius with machinery, his long experience had taught him to detect the slightest change in the mood of the engine. To me the noise of those engines seemed deafening, but to Harry's ears it was a kind of music. I should perhaps explain that when the flywheel picked up speed after being started, the explosions emitted increased until they occurred at the rate of about two per second. The engines were all fitted with silencers but, in my opinion, these didn't seem to make much difference and only Harry could find anything to appreciate in their steady beat. What was remarkable was the way Harry sub-consciously tuned in to the rhythm of the engines and could hear the most subtle change of beat long before anyone else. No matter where he happened to be, even if it was in some distant corner of the wheel, his ear could always sense if one of the engines was about to go wrong. The sight of Harry scampering through the yard, followed more sedately by his assistant Ernest, was often the first indication to the rest of us that trouble was afoot with one of the engines.

One day the baby engine suddenly went berserk. First it seemed to slow to a virtual standstill, then it let loose a mighty explosion, finally, and without warning, it began rotating backwards! It was fortunate that the engine did not drive any of the grinding wheels, for the consequences might have been catastrophic. The history of Sheffield's grinding trade is littered with tales of disasters caused by sudden engine reversals. When the engines function properly, the grindstones in the workshop rotate away from the grinder sitting on his horsing and, in doing so, they tighten on the axle. However, a reversing engine means a reversing stone, and it only takes a few backward spins for the stone to break free from its axle. Then the furiously spinning stone will head straight towards the grinder—many a man has been maimed or killed by a flying stone. Some of the walls in the old wheels bore the marks left by stones which had smashed into them following the sudden reversal of an engine.

This particular engine at Moseley's only drove some buffs, but it could still have provoked a very serious accident. Fortunately, old Harry got to the switch very quickly and stopped the engine. Naturally, the alarm had brought work to a halt in the adjoining shops and everybody rushed to inspect the scene of the trouble. We were relieved to see that nobody had been injured, and then simply fell about laughing when we saw that the reversing buffs had ejected all manner of muck and filth from the troughs and splattered it all over the faces and overalls of every polisher and buffer in sight!

The engine which served our workshop had an 18-foot flywheel and thankfully, in my time, it never displayed the tantrums of its baby brother. The power from the engine was transmitted by a series of line shafting, pulleys and leather belting which passed through walls, floors and ceilings to serve the upper and lower rooms. In our case the line shafting was below the level of the floor, there were three drum wheels, each about five feet deep and three feet wide, sunk into specially created pits built into the ground, each drum served two grinding troughs. Considering the steel girders that reinforced the ceiling, the pulleys and leather belting, the workshop invariably seemed somewhat congested and cluttered, also bearing in mind that the area behind our five troughs was filled with machinery and equipment for other processes (all using the same source of power), it is evident that there wasn't much free space.

The belts which fed the power directly to the grindstones have figured prominently in the folklore of grinding, it was these which were often stolen or destroyed in the days when rattening was rife in the grinding trade. A grinder is helpless without his belt. The belts, which passed through part of an old tree trunk, known as a 'bearstake', on the way to the pulley which turned the grindstone, were about three inches wide and probably 72 feet long when new; but, of course, they were worked hard and long and were

Sheffield grinders in action.

A corner of a grinding wheel showing line shafting, buffs and leather belting, or bands.

Years of wear from the belt cut deep grooves into the wooden bearstakes.

seldom replaced until they literally dropped to pieces. Frequently shortened to suit the ever-diminishing size of the grindstones, then lengthened when a new stone was fitted, these constant adjustments, coupled with the normal wear and tear and repairs, usually left the patched belts looking neglected and primitive, but it was not the way of a grinder to invest in costly new equipment unless it was absolutely necessary.

I soon learned that while the grinders of Sheffield were a jolly and generous breed, especially if you met them on Saint Monday, they were also rather tight-fisted when it came to putting their hands in their pockets to pay for essentials. They found it painful enough paying the rent. On Tuesdays, after the previous day's free-spending on booze, I've seen Dad count his few remaining coppers and then disappear to ensure missing Moseley's secretary, Mr Collier, when he called to collect the rent. Moreover, I've known many instances where men have persisted with equipment that ought to have been replaced, constantly pleading poverty as the reason. When they were left with no choice but obtain replacements, the old grinders invariably made their purchases on the never-never if the equipment was new, or they bought second-hand goods.

This reminds me of a tale Dad once told me about an incident at one grinding wheel he had known in his youth. Apparently, one weekend, the place was gutted by fire and had to be completely rebuilt. The insurance money enabled the owner to re-equip the wheel with entirely new machinery and fittings. The grinders were delighted—but it didn't take them long to turn the situation to advantage. Removing what equipment they could, they sold it to a local dealer and used the cash to obtain second-hand replacements. They then shared out the profits. Dad claimed that the owner was never any the wiser—and the grinders launched into one of the booziest Saint Mondays they had ever known!

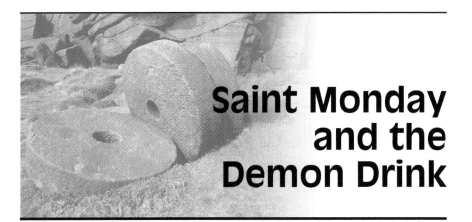

Saint Monday and the Demon Drink

The cutlery craftsmen of Sheffield always had a fondness for the boozer. Dad was typical of his breed and, such was his liking for his pint of ale, that he invariably called for what he described as 'a livener' on his way to work at the start of the day—imagine dropping into a pub before half-past eight in the morning! He had to use the back door of course, but he was seldom alone in his breakfast-time boozing.

Against this background, the first part of my initiation into the world of grinding, was an introduction to the ritual of Saint Monday on my very first day at the wheel. That morning I did very little work, but then, neither did anyone else! As soon as the pub officially opened, Dad would take everybody down there. Some of my new colleagues were probably what was called 'drunken badly' on Monday mornings anyway, still feeling thick-headed after their weekend exploits. They would drift into the wheel looking rather glum and still half-asleep, for an hour or two they would potter about doing very little. Then, as opening time approached, they would begin to liven up and at the appropriate signal off they would start for the pub.

The streets would be suddenly filled with grinders, buffer girls and others, all heading for the pubs of the district. Everyone in the local trades believed in the custom of Saint Monday, and some were so keen to start the action that they formed queues on the pub steps long before the doors were opened. The ritual involved remaining in the pub until closing time, meanwhile drinking, singing, talking, laughing, playing cards and even dancing, just as if it were Saturday night. Few of them ever went home sober—and I know there were at least two occasions in my experience when Dad's condition caused him to lose his driving licence because he insisted on using his car to travel home.

Our local was the Great Britain, a beerhouse in John Street also known as The Ship. Every room in the place would be packed within minutes of opening time. Though not unfamiliar with public houses, I was astonished to

Great Britain, *John Street, also known as* The Ship.

Some of the Saint Monday drinkers. Herbert senior and his brother Joe are 3rd and 5th from the left.

find that, as a lad of fourteen just beginning his career in cutlery, my presence did not arouse any comment. 'If tha'rt going to be a grinder, lad,' somebody might have said, 'tha's got to learn to participate in the booze-ups on Saint Monday'. As you might expect, few of the grinders wanted to leave at closing time, and many of the landlords continued to serve beer long after hours. There were few Mondays when Dad left the Great Britain before tea-time. However, I remember one day when he and his pals had to make a hasty exit during a police raid. There they were, noisily playing cards—solo was their favourite game—when someone shouted 'the cops are here!' Dad can never have moved so quickly—in a moment, every member of that card school shot through a window and made his escape via the backyard. The irony of the incident was that one of the group who escaped wasn't a grinder at all. He was an off-duty police inspector attached to Sheffield's Flying Squad!

Those Saint Monday sessions were jolly occasions and, fortunately, most of the grinders and buffer girls were able to make up for lost time during the rest of the week. When they wanted to, the grinders could buckle down and really graft from Tuesday to Saturday. However, there were a few who boozed to excess and believed that every day was a Saint's day. They were in a minority but, ironically, they were often amongst the finest craftsmen of their time, in fact, Dad's oldest and best grinder, Ernest Machin, was a classic example of this type.

Old Ernest must have been about sixty when I first knew him; a friendly man with snowy white hair, a straight and proud stance, a twinkle in his eyes and always a smile on his face. He liked to pull my leg and told many stories about his days as a boxer. He always claimed to have fought and beaten the local champion, Johnny Cuthbert, long before Johnny gained a Lonsdale Belt. I never knew if this was true, though I did confirm that he and Cuthbert had been lads together. Ernest always wore a pair of torn overalls which looked as if they had never been washed and, if he didn't work as fast as the others, he was undisputedly the best grinder in our wheel, the quality of his grinding put him in a class of his own. The trouble was, if Ernest had any money in his pocket, he wouldn't come to work. Leaving his little two-roomed house in Hammond Street, he would make straight for the nearest pub, and only when he had spent up would he remember that he was expected at the wheel.

In those days the men who worked for Dad were all on piecework, being paid so much a dozen for the blades they ground. A system of 'sweets' and 'sours' was in operation. That is, if things went well and a man had earned a good wage, he could, if he wished, defer payment on some of the work until the following week. The blades on which payment was deferred were known as 'sweets'. On the other hand if things had gone badly for a chap, if for any reason he had lost a lot of time, he could claim against work not yet done.

The blades on which he collected advance payment were known as 'sours'. Poor old Ernest, he was permanently on sours! He would be forever promising 'I'll start working them off tomorrow' but he seldom seemed to manage it. Dad, being fond of Ernest, was immensely patient with him, which must have been difficult when there was a rush job on. However, it would not have been easy for Dad to criticise Ernest's love of the pub, it would have been like having the kettle call the pot black! Dad sought to compromise by calling to collect Ernest on the way to work, as that seemed to be the only way of ensuring that his best grinder made it to the wheel on time! Sometimes, however, Ernest would disappear for weeks at a time. My last memories were of his final days. The poor chap eventually died of cancer, but even when he was ill he would come down to the wheel, deliver his sick note, and then sit on the steps outside waiting to go for a drink with Dad.

Bill Turner, probably the finest craftsman I ever knew.

Another man for whom drink was his downfall was Bill Turner, one of the finest craftsmen I ever saw. A tall, slim man of great strength, he was a hand forger who worked exclusively for Moseley's and to see him in action in his little smither's shop was a wonderful experience. Moseley's supplied Bill with eight-foot lengths of double sheer steel from which he forged all types of trade knife blades in a variety of sizes. I once watched him hand forge a 14-inch butcher's knife (about 20 inches long in total) and I was transfixed with admiration—it was sheer poetry. With one blow he cut the steel to the required length. Then he began to heat up one end of the metal in his blacksmith's hearth, one hand holding the bar in a pair of tongs while he used the other hand to pump the pigskin bellows. When the steel was white hot he hammered it into the required shape, then, after shaping the first few inches of the point of the blade, he would turn to the tang and choil (the part where the blade edge meets the handle) finally giving attention to the middle part of the knife. After that the forged blade was hardened and tempered by being re-heated and dipped in water. From start to finish, the entire operation was completed with a speed and simplicity which made the task seem deceptively easy but even as a lad I knew I was in the presence of a man of rare strength and skill.

Alas, the demon drink haunted Bill, you never knew when he would disappear on one of his benders. It was said that when he'd had a few drinks he experienced a sudden character change, and it was tough luck on anyone who crossed him at such times. He had a large family of children and it was common knowledge that he was in the habit of rough treating his wife whenever he slipped into a drunken rage. Because of his drunkenness, from time to time, Bill would end up in court and get sent to prison for a couple of months. When he returned to work after one of these spells, he would seem like a reformed man, dried out and apparently determined to stay sober. At these times you could not imagine there was a milder person in the whole of Sheffield; and his wife would often call at the wheel, no doubt checking that he was keeping his promise to lay off the booze.

Unfortunately, these quiet periods seldom lasted. If Bill was seen in the pub on Saint Monday it was often a warning that he was ready to go on another bender. It always seemed to me a terrible waste of talent, and I could never understand why a man with such wonderful abilities could allow himself to be the victim of such self-destruction. Of course, I was still very young then and I had a lot to learn about life. I think I learned to accept Bill for what he was, and I remember him now with great affection, but I think that seeing what was happening to him served to teach me one lesson I took to heart. It might be all right to enjoy myself on Saint Monday, but it would never pay to let the booze become my master.

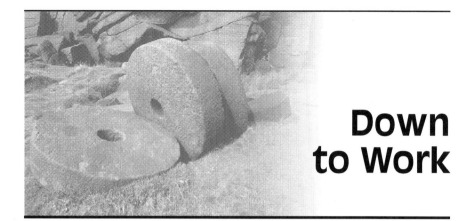

Down to Work

After my introduction to the custom of Saint Monday on my first day at Moseley's Wheel, I probably thought it was a jolly way of life being a grinder. However, I soon realised that, in truth, the merrymaking which marked the start of the working week was merely a footnote to the business that really mattered, and life from Tuesday to Saturday was mostly a very serious and sober affair!

The business of H. Housley, Grinder, handled a wide range of knife blades—butchers' knives, bread knives, carving knives, solid (monoblock) army knives, ham and beef slicers—most of the work was in carbon steel. The workforce had to get through a lot of grinding to make it pay, it was necessary to process more than 1,000 dozen knife blades a week to earn a living. In those days Dad had a team of eight or nine, five of whom were skilled grinders. He would collect perhaps thirty gross of blanks at a time, then share them out amongst the five grinders, the quantities he gave each depended on the speed at which each man could work. The others in the team usually completed the various supplementary operations. Dad himself might do some grinding if, for instance, Ernest Machin failed to turn up but he often concentrated on blade buffing or adapted to meet particular circumstances.

The workshop contained three rows of equipment: the main grinding was done on the 60-inch diameter grindstones in the five troughs in front; tumbling or side glazing on the large leather covered buffs immediately behind; and neck grinding and blade buffing on equipment on the back row.

Of course, in those days, for me it was very much a case of adjusting to my new surroundings. The first priority was to pick up a few basics, try to get to know what was going on around me, and to seek to make myself useful. Despite all my fears, I soon felt at home. Perhaps the early visit to the pub had removed a few inhibitions but, anyway, the women wanted to mother me and the men were keen to see that I learned my way around. I was in a

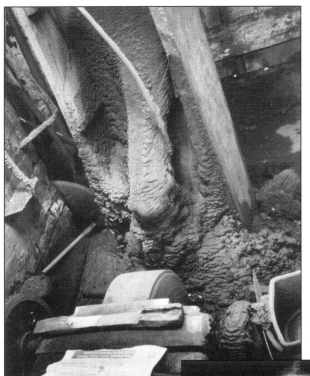

Build up of swarf on the splashboard of a grinding trough.

Brian Alcock, a contemporary grinder, at Beehive Works, Milton Street.

grown-up, down-to-earth world, and soon recognised that the others were ready to treat me as an adult and seldom as a fourteen-year-old boy.

I have to admit that, in the beginning, my enthusiasm and keenness to impress didn't always have the desired effect, and the results of my boyish willingness sometimes brought a smile to the faces of my older colleagues, in fact the very first task I undertook left me blushing with embarrassment. I was asked to make a wheelbarrow, it seemed such an easy challenge that I couldn't imagine it presenting a problem. So, when I went into the drying room, formerly a small hardening shop, to begin the job, I knew I was going to make the biggest and best barrow my new mates had ever seen. Finding some cast-iron wheels and large planking, I was soon deeply engrossed and, when I finished, I was so proud of my handiwork the others had to be invited to inspect it. Murmurs of respectful approbation fell upon my ears, but my bubble of pride suddenly burst—when I tried to get the barrow through the door it was too big! Amidst laughter which left me blushing, I hastily removed the wheels and shafting and set about reassembling my masterpiece on the other side of the narrow doorway!

Soon afterwards I was given the chance to begin my formal education as a grinder, starting by learning to master the comparatively simple, but nevertheless sometimes painful, art of neck grinding—a job usually given to beginners and done on a dry and very narrow grindstone about half-an-inch wide. A reason the job of neck grinding was given to a beginner, apart from the obvious one of giving him experience, was that if he didn't get it absolutely right the grinder who followed him could correct any faults.

I should, perhaps, explain that only forged blades with integral bolsters have necks, the neck being that part of the blade which slopes up to the bolster. These bolsters come in a wide range of shapes and sizes, and I found that in grinding the necks it was necessary to vary the shape of the edge on the narrow grindstone. Thus, though the grinding of the blade itself involved putting pressure down onto the full face of the grindstone, neck grinding required the slope of the bolster to be pulled or pressed against the side of the stone, using both hands to exert pressure and, at the same time, controlling the movements to ensure the entire area of the neck was ground. Until a grinder acquired full control, the blade constantly slipped over the edge of the stone. Being, as yet, unskilled I kept catching a finger or thumb on the revolving stone. A wound caused by a grindstone not only cuts but burns and, though seldom serious, it was certainly very painful—and it didn't help that my cries of anguish were invariably greeted by howls of laughter from workmates!

The blade being processed was in a black-hardened state, having under-gone heat treatment after forging. Any dirt or scale stamped into the red hot steel during forging created small depressions. Grinding removed the bulk of these but some tiny pits and holes known as 'blacks' remained along the, as yet, imperfect surface. After grinding, the knife went forward for neck glazing and the removal of blacks, this was done on a narrow leather-covered buff which was coated with glue and emery.

By the time I had begun to find neck grinding a little less painful, I had been introduced to another operation known as 'o'er rolling'—a further step in the process of becoming familiar with the feel of the grindstone. A knife blade is quite thick when it arrives from the forge, and so the larger blades were given a preliminary grind called o'er rolling before passing to the skilled grinder who provided the fine-finishing skills. It was not just a question of reducing the thickness of the blade, however, the task also involved putting on an initial taper and the beginnings of an edge. This taper was important, as a correctly ground blade tapers from neck to point and from back to edge.

I soon found out that the skilled grinder who took my 'completed' work did not like correcting my mistakes. It was at this stage that I recognised that part of the learning process involved accepting criticism. Those old Sheffield grinders could tell at a glance if a piece of work was inferior. Indeed they didn't need or use any measuring instruments. A grinder simply relied on his trained eye to judge the correct accuracy and springiness of a blade, and the finest exponents of the art of blade grinding could make the edge of a blade 'lift'. Prior to the advent of stainless steel, best quality trade-knife blades were hand forged from fine quality double shear steel. A skilled blade forger, such as Bill Turner, could harden and temper a blade so skilfully that even if it was bent double it would spring back to absolute straightness. One day, when I was about fifteen, curiosity about this theory overcame me. At the time I was fine-glazing some sixteen-inch, narrow, ham-slicer blades. Taking the tip of the blade I formed a loop, passing the tip through the loop I formed a figure of eight with the blade and showed it to the rest of the grinders. On reversing the procedure, the blade assumed, perfectly, its original shape. A skilled hand grinder could make the edge of a blade actually 'lift', indeed some manufacturers demanded that trade knife blade edges should be 'ground to lift'. To make a blade lift, the edge of the blade was pressed down onto the thumb nail and when pressure was released the edge would spring back to a straight edge. By drawing the edge of a knife blade across his thumb, and at the same time exerting pressure with the other hand, the grinder could detect any places along the edge where the blade failed to lift. Further grinding would follow until the blade lifted along its entire length—a certain way of ensuring wonderful sharpness. Many Sheffield grinders bore tell-tale cuts on their thumb nail from testing for lift. In the face of such skilled craftsmanship, and dealing with men who had great faith in their own

Jack Wild working on a double heading machine in 1988.

A blade buff, leather covered and dressed with glue and emery.

abilities, I found them not always patient with the errors of beginners; it was rather a chastening experience to hear one's efforts condemned! However, I gradually improved, and I also progressed to become an expert at 'double-heading', and at dressing the double-heading glazers.

After normal grinding all knives used to be fine ground on a whittening stone—a very hard grindstone of extra-fine grit which removed very little metal but smoothed out the rough grinding marks left by the coarse grindstone. At the time of my arrival on the scene, there were two alternatives to whittening: tumbling and double-heading. At our wheel we preferred the latter.

Tumbling was a very similar operation to whittening in that the blade was placed in a 'flatstick' and rubbed vigorously up, down and across the face of the revolving tumbler glazer—the tumbler being a large wooden wheel three feet in diameter and eight inches wide, the surface of which was covered by thick leather from a bull's neck or hide of a walrus. This leather had been coated in hot glue and the tumbler rolled in an abrasive such as emery or aloxite of a suitable grit size to give the desired smooth finish to the blade.

A double-headed glazing wheel was made of steel, being about 20 inches in diameter and two inches wide, and on the outside was fitted a three-inch cushion of compressed calico segments called 'divine wheels'. The wheels were dressed with a mixture of glue and emery in the form of a hot paste which was literally painted on with an ordinary paint brush—I quickly mastered the art of doing this dressing.

However, I wasn't always quite so adept at using the double-header itself. As its name implies, the equipment comprised two wheels which revolved inwards towards each other, and the idea was to pass the blade in between the two glazers. Unfortunately, I didn't always get my timing right, and once, when I was putting some army knives through the process, I was rather premature in using my foot to bring the wheels together; the knife I was holding was dragged from my grasp and finished up stuck in my knee—I still carry the scar today.

Apart from the inherent dangers of lapses in co-ordination between hand and foot on the double-heading glazer, or losing control whilst doing neck grinding, perhaps the most common source of discomfort in the wheel was to get a mote in the eye. Horace Broadhead, who was our expert at removing these tiny particles of steel, always called them 'moyts'. Horace made himself a small magnet lance which he used to remove the motes, and he always said that if they came out within a few hours they were no trouble. Unfortunately, you didn't always know that you'd got a mote in your eye— yet if you left one in overnight it would become covered by a thin film of skin, and then it could prove really troublesome. Horace was skilled at nicking this film of skin, but always declined to do so if the mote was close to the pupil. 'You'd better go to the hospital,' he would say; but the truth was, that because the hospital didn't deal in mote removing as often as Horace, they were never quite as skilled at it. Many a man returned to the wheel complaining about the mess the medical experts had made of the job!

As I have said, my early months at the wheel were a time when I displayed great enthusiasm, always anxious to please and impress my colleagues. I especially wanted to satisfy Dad—and in this I succeeded for the most part. Then one day, when I gave him an unexpected dose of pain, my rating sank to rock bottom and he didn't talk to me for weeks! In the drying room where we hung the glazers after they had been dressed, we aided the drying process with some metal sheet covering which was kept in place with an old heavy grindstone axle. Dad must have called in to see what I was doing and, in my haste to show him the fruits of my labour, I accidentally knocked over the axle which crashed straight onto his foot.

For years afterwards he had trouble with that foot, and at the time of the incident he certainly let me know what he thought of me. It was painful just to see him limping along and pulling a face which told me I was out of favour. When Dad was upset or annoyed with someone he was always pointedly silent in their presence—and I got the silent treatment for a long time. However, if Dad was sometimes not on speaking terms, I seldom had any trouble persuading the others to talk. My colleagues at the wheel, not only in our workshop, were a lively lot, and I remember them all not only with great affection but with a clarity which is still as vivid as ever, even after almost sixty years.

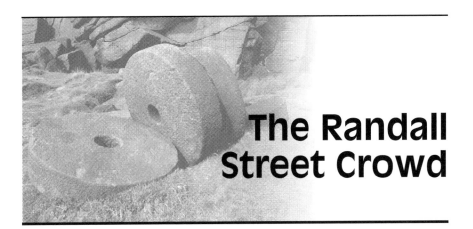

The Randall Street Crowd

The grinders of Sheffield were both unique and special—a breed apart. Independent, proud, sometimes a trifle eccentric, and always slightly suspicious of outsiders, but they were the salt of the earth, the greatest people in the world. It was a wonderful experience for a young lad to be a part of that close-knit community in which such an excellent *esprit de corps* existed.

Moseley's Wheel was typical of hundreds of similar cutlery premises in the area, I shall always remember it as a place filled with many great and colourful characters who taught me not only my trade but about life. In truth, a grinding wheel was a grey place, but those people made the workaday world of my youth seem bright and lively and they filled it with laughter and incident.

Dad's team comprised Ernest Machin, Sammy Short, Harold and Horace Broadhead, Sam Moseley, Sarah Cheetham, Edith Ness and Alice Shaw—just to list the names brings back a flood of memories. Add to this group all those others based elsewhere in the wheel, or who were associated with it, and you have a crowd whose separate stories provide a panoramic insight into the working world of Sheffield's cutlery trade at the end of the 1930s.

Of Dad's group I have already referred to the best of the grinders, Ernest Machin, and though I have said he was the slowest, perhaps, on reflection, that distinction belonged to Sammy Short. Sammy, however, could not match Ernest in terms of quality and, while Ernest always wore a smile, Sammy had the most mournful expression I have ever seen on a man's face. Sammy suffered with piles, which may have accounted for his perpetually miserable look; and in his discomfort he always had sympathy, for it cannot have helped that he had to sit at his trough on uncomfortable horsing in a damp, wet workshop every day of his working life. His painful condition may also have explained his slowness; though, in truth, I fancy that as a bachelor in the veteran stage of his life he didn't feel either the need or the

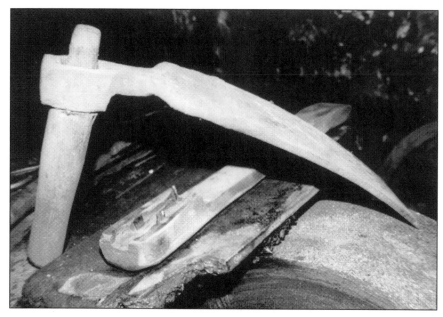

A hack hammer, used to dress the grindstone to improve it's cutting power. Under it is a flatstick used by the grinder to hold and control the blade being ground.

inclination to work fast, for he could earn as much as his circumstances required.

Harold Broadhead, on the other hand, always had the reputation of being the quickest grinder in Dad's team. Known as 'Curly' and looking a bit like Charlie Chaplin with his bushy black hair and a little moustache, he was then in his early twenties, and I think his weekly wage averaged £5, which was good money then. The trouble with Harold was that he was always in too much of a hurry. A man was supposed to keep his grindstone flat, and avoid wearing it down on one side; but Harold's was invariably at an angle, for he never had the time to bother readjusting it. Dad always used to say 'Harold's scuffling again—I wish the lad would stop rushing and give himself time to do the job properly'. When the finished blades were sent to the warehouse, you could bet that most of the ones rejected would be Harold's. So, although he was quick, his speed was misleading; it was very much a case of more haste, less speed. In those days, by the way, the grinders never referred to work as having been rejected: if your blades were returned it was said 'tha's got cuckoo for that job'. Harold often got cuckoo, yet whatever his shortcomings in his early days, he eventually became his own boss, and his brother, Horace, also eventually set up as a Little Mester.

The women who worked for Dad were a lively trio of double-headers— Sarah Cheetham, Edith Ness and Alice Shaw. Perhaps Alice, who worked alongside me on one of the double-heading machines in a separate little workshop, was the quietest of the three but Sarah and Edith made up for it.

Sarah, a spinster, was like an all-in wrestler in build, a small, chunky, rosy-cheeked woman in her thirties, with shoulders like Rocky Marciano. She was as strong as an ox and, in most respects, absolutely without fear. Most of her days were passed in a constant bubble of laughter, but, she was terrified of mice—the sight of one was enough to reduce her to tearful helplessness. Edith was a widow with two young boys, and it must have been quite a trial for her having to run a home and turn out to work. Yet she was a bundle of fun, and it was her comical antics which provoked much of Sarah's laughter. Edith was always up to some prank or other and she had plenty of opportunity with Dad often absent from the wheel—usually at the pub. I remember one day when Dad was out, Edith picked up his battered old trilby, put it on her head, and proceeded to give a wonderful imitation of the Old Man. With all the appropriate gestures, she mimicked Dad's way of handing out work. 'Thee do them blades there, Harold, and now then, Ernest, thee do them. And when tha's done them, tha'd better do these.' The voice was perfect, and we all fell about laughing, until somebody noticed that Dad had returned and was standing in the open doorway taking note of the performance!

There was another occasion when Sarah Cheetham and Sammy Short provided a similarly spontaneous 'entertainment'. Sammy was suffering from a septic finger which kept him off work and when he came in with his panel note he was wearing his Sunday suit. It so happened that someone had brought Sarah a bunch of home-grown flowers, she picked these up and went over to Sammy. 'I see you're dressed for the wedding, Sam' and, taking his arm, they walked down the workshop together, her humming loudly 'Here Comes the Bride'. Even Sammy's normally deadpan expression broke into a smile, but just then, Dad walked in. He didn't speak, but the look on his face spoke volumes; and Sarah and Sammy shuffled quietly away.

Yes, Sarah and Edith were a grand pair, women in a man's world but the equal of any man. They could outshine many when it came to blunt speaking and the use of earthy language. Yet both were warm and generous, and content to mother me. I shall never forget how they helped me celebrate my first Christmas at the wheel. They insisted on taking me to the Queen Adelaide pub, in Bramall Lane, where they fed me on port. I must have drunk about ten glasses before closing time, and then Sarah and Edith all but carried me to the tram stop. Somehow I got home—I crawled up Portland Street to our house on my hands and knees. When I returned to work after the holiday, the women asked if I'd had a good Christmas, but I had to confess that I could barely remember—it had taken me three days to emerge from the depths of my hangover.

Elsewhere in the wheel there were more rare characters, from 'Owd' Ben, the veteran grinder who could not resist a chat and joke, to old Wingfield, Moseley's grinding shop foreman, who never smiled and was never seen to pass the time of day with anyone except to issue instructions. Ben was at that stage in his career when, his heavy grinding days behind him, he was content to pass his time on lighter work. Thus he was the only person I every saw doing side glazing—the practice had already virtually died out. This was a form of polishing which put 'colour' into blades. The coarse grinding marks had already been removed by whittening and then blades were buffed using finer and finer grades of emery. Finally a side glazer, with no abrasive, was used. This was coated with a greasy compound and the blade being polished was moved rapidly to and fro across the glazer. The process imparted a fine sheen, referred to as 'colour', to the previously dull steel. The boss would say 'Gi' it some elbow grease an' get some colour in it'.

I think Ben, then turned 70, had plenty of time on his hands, and so he would wander about the place launching into conversations wherever he could find a willing listener. However I seldom heard him say anything serious, for his talk was one long string of daft jokes, and his sense of humour was absolutely zany. It seemed childish, really, yet you couldn't help but laugh. Only many years later did I realise that Ben's crazy brand of comedy was a forerunner of that which ultimately brought The Goons such great popularity.

There were two self-employed hardeners on the premises, though Snicker Jepson and Ernest Harrison were known to everybody as 'hotters and cowders' (colders) which I suppose described the hardening process. Snicker, who smoked Black Cat cigarettes, was the bookie's runner in the wheel, which meant he was sometimes the most popular man on the place and sometimes not. Dad being a compulsive gambler, no doubt had plenty of dealings with Snicker. For my part, I was closer to Ernest Harrison, the other hardener. Known as 'Birdy', he was a great talker, a genuine raconteur and in me he found a ready and eager listener.

In those days I often had a lot of spare time. One of my jobs, dressing the glazers, involved a good deal of waiting about—first while the glue boiled, then while the glazers dried between each coating of glue and emery. So I found it convenient to listen to Birdy Harrison's reminiscences. Some sixteen years earlier in his career he had spent a period working in the Irish Free State in the days when there were moves to establish a cutlery and other industries over there following independence. Birdy had been one of about thirty craftsmen sent over from Sheffield to Newbridge, where they converted an old cavalry barracks into a factory. The few years he had spent there were a constant source of inspiration to Birdy, and he happily talked for hours about 'the bit of paradise' that had been his home; recalling the beauties of the Irish countryside and wonderful salmon fishing he had enjoyed in idyllic surroundings close by his workshop.

Fishing was the favourite pastime of most grinders, I had been introduced to it very early in life. Dad was a very enthusiastic fisherman and taught me to fish when we went to Boston for holidays during my boyhood; so it was natural that I should get into the habit of joining him on excursions into Lincolnshire in later years.

I remember one very pleasant character Dad met through fishing. Jack Harrison was not in the grinding trade, but he was a frequent caller at the Great Britain pub where we held our Saint Monday sessions. I think he was one of those chaps who moved about trading in all manner of things, but my outstanding memory is of the day he was delivering his sales patter about a revolutionary new fishing rod which he described as being the greatest thing ever invented in angling history. I think he said the rod was made of fibreglass. 'You can do anything with it', he said. 'Why, you can bend it double and it won't break'. To illustrate his point he began to set up the rod. Unfortunately, he forgot that the pub had a very low ceiling, and as he extended the rod above his head it met resistance and began to bend. Just as he was assuring us that it was unbreakable, the rod snapped in half. Jack beat a hasty exit amid gales of laughter.

Fishing reminds me of one of the most unforgettable characters I ever met in the grinding trades, Frank Booth was his name. Though he didn't work at Moseley's Wheel, he was in the army during the time I was there, he was a good pal of Dad's, so consequently I often came into contact with him in later years when we went fishing. Frank was not a big man, but very strong, as hard as nails and fearless; a man's man and more—not the kind of chap you would wish to provoke if you cared for your good looks.

In those days Jeffcock's used to run fishing trips every Saturday and Sunday, and Frank went on them twice every weekend for many years. The coach used to stand by the bridge on Blonk Street waiting to collect the fishermen, the journey was so arranged that the men would be dropped at various points along the Trent or the Witham, from where they were collected later. One Sunday morning Frank turned up as usual only to be told by Jeffcock 'Sorry, Frank, the bus is full'. Frank's face immediately registered the blackness of thunder, and I'm sure the ground beneath his feet trembled. The language he used in telling Jeffcock what he thought of him was probably the bluest the coach proprietor had ever heard. Then, when

Frank had used up his entire vocabulary of swearwords, he suddenly grabbed hold of Jeffcock and hung him by his coat on the bridge railings before turning around and marching away!

It was some time after the war when Frank started going fishing with Dad and me, and when we witnessed an incident which not only said a lot about Frank but provided a classic example of the typical attitude of the old school of Sheffield grinders. I have already referred to Dad's unconscious selfishness, but even Dad wasn't as totally immersed in his own life and needs as Frank. We had arranged to pick him up at his home at half-past five one Sunday morning. When we arrived, Frank was just coming out of the front door, this was unusual because we sometimes had to knock him up. 'You'll have to hang on a minute' he said, 'I've just got to go and telephone the midwife.' In the previous year, Frank, a long-time bachelor of 45, had married a young widow. We had known that Mrs Booth was expecting their first child but, until that moment, we had no idea that the birth was so close at hand. Dad said 'But Frank, you're not going to go off and leave the Missis to have the baby while you're away fishing, are you?' Frank admitted that was his plan 'She'll be all right, tha knows'. It took us at least ten minutes to persuade our pal that, in the circumstances, his place was at home, and it was only with considerable reluctance that Frank gave up his fishing expedition.

Typically, the next time we saw him he was more concerned about the fish he had missed catching than talking about the birth of his child!

John Street Interlude

I n 1942, soon after the start of my third year at the grinding wheel, changes occurred which altered the direction of my cutlery career. The war continued and the situation at work was that there was plenty to be done but not always enough people with the skills to do it. As a sub-contractor Dad got ample regular work from a half-dozen or more firms, and he had no difficulty reorganising to handle the extra demand for grinding. In fact, at about this time he was able to bring his brother, my Uncle Joe, back into the trade. Uncle Joe had started out as a grinder but, later, in consequence of various circumstances, had ended up working as a dustman with the Sheffield Cleansing Department. No doubt he was pleased to return to his proper trade, and Dad welcomed him with open arms.

Dad's calls at the local warehouses alerted him to an intriguing situation. In a time when business was booming, the manufacturers were managing to get all the extra knife-grinding done, but a shortage of skilled labour meant the later processes were creating bottle-necks which slowed down completion of the finished products, such as the army knives which were then in such great demand. Worried manufacturers often asked Dad 'Do you know anybody who can do us any buffing or cutling, Herbert?' So it wasn't long before Dad saw an opportunity for him to expand his operation. One day he revealed plans to rent additional premises at Truswell's property in John Street—just a stone's throw from Moseley's Wheel. I was delighted for him, but didn't know the development would mean a move for me, until Dad explained that he was building up a new team which he wanted me to join.

So, I spent the next eighteen months in a set-up which was very different from that which I had previously known. Now the operations included spoon and fork buffing, hafting, cutling, knife serrating, knife handle finishing, mirror polishing and more. The move suited me, not just because I welcomed the chance to learn about other aspects of production, but by

A page from my father's accounts book, 1941. Wizard Abrasives supplied the five grindstones leased by my father for £3 2s 6d a week. H. Stamps were National Health Stamps to cover the nine employees — £1 11s 3d. IT was income tax deducted. My wages, H.H.Jnr, were 16s 0d for a 5½ day week.

virtue of the opportunity presented to increase my income. Having earned sixteen shillings per week (80p) at the grinding wheel, I managed to step up to just over £4 a week once I had mastered all the jobs I was required to do at the new place—and that kind of money was an excellent wage for a teenager then.

Unfortunately, the start to the new era was marred by a tragedy involving a young woman who was going to work for Dad and an independent grinder from one of the two adjoining wheels. The woman, though set on as a buffer, volunteered to help Dad with the task of getting the John Street workshop ready and, while spindles were being set up and benches built, the walls were whitewashed. An excellent worker who seemed certain to become a very useful member of the new team, she got on well with everybody, and got into the habit of spending her tea breaks standing near the fire in one of the other wheels. On the day of the tragedy she went, as usual, to mash a pot of tea next door. Waiting for the kettle to boil, she was standing talking with someone when suddenly a nearby grindstone burst. The impact of the explosion threw the grinder, Frank Depledge, and his horsing backwards and he finished up twenty yards away on some drumboards; but a section of the shattered stone flew across the room and struck the woman on the head. I believe the force of the blow killed her instantly. Frank suffered severe bruising and was left to reflect on how lucky he had been to escape so lightly. However, the incident caused him to completely lose his nerve, and he never worked in a grinding wheel again.

As I have said, with the war on, the greatest demand was for the solid-handled army knives and at John Street we had a part to play in producing these. Up the road at Randall Street, Dad and his team ground and glazed the blades, and we were left to deal with the handles. These handles had previously been hot forged and left scaled black, to grind away this blackness we used a small pedestal grinder which had a stone twelve inches in diameter and two inches wide. We then removed the grinding marks, using the glazer dressed in the normal way with glue and emery abrasive, and after an initial glaze the handles were given a finer glaze.

We concentrated largely on handles rather than blades, but we did also perform back glazing, which was cleaning up the backs of the blades; and we also dealt with serrating the blade edges if this was required. Serrating was done on a 14-inch diameter dry grindstone 1½ inches wide. The real skill was not so much in the grinding but in preparing the grindstone, for a diamond cutting tool had to be used to create hollows in the stone to produce the serrated edge when the blade was presented to the face of the stone.

Serrating a knife blade.

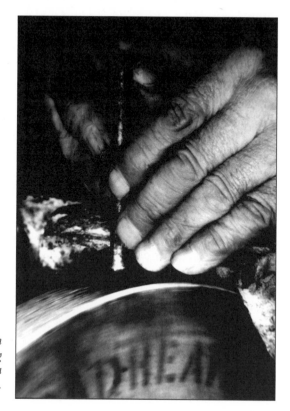

To make a serrating wheel, an industrial diamond is being used to cut grooves into a grindstone.

After my experience in knife-making, the range of operations in Dad's new workshop gave me an insight into aspects of the production of spoons and forks, particularly buffing, insiding, graining and dollying. Before buffing all the spoons and forks were filed, though, in truth, the term 'filed' was a bit of a misnomer. In earlier years this job was done by hand but, by my time, it had become a machine operation. However, those who did the job of removing the flash from the edges of the spoons and forks continued to be called filers, though they actually worked on a very fine grindstone—hand filing only survived in the production of solid silver spoons and forks.

Buffing, and the women who did this rather unpleasant job, have passed into the folklore of Sheffield's cutlery industry. They were indeed a rare and colourful breed; jolly lasses, earthy characters invariably full of life but always loveable. If they earned good money it was because they deserved it, for they were both skilful and very hardworking. I think it will be of interest to explain some details of the buffing process, by which imperfections were removed from spoons and forks as they were given a smooth surface.

To buff a spoon required working on both surfaces of the handle, back and front, the edges of the handle, the rim of the bowl, and the back and inside of the bowl. The majority of these operations could be completed on a 10–12 inch diameter buff. This wooden buff had a leather cover which was treated with resin to give it a suitable surface. The melting of the resin in a small ladle held over a gas ring invariably filled the workshop with smoke, so you always knew when someone was preparing to buff, and I soon noticed that whilst resin was being melted the buffer usually took time to mix together some special buffing sand and engine oil. Then if, for instance, she was buffing the handle, edges, rim or back of the bowl of a spoon, she would pick up perhaps half a dozen spoons in one hand, and with the other she would scoop up a handful of the oily damp sand, then, bringing both hands together, she presented one spoon and the sand together to the buff, this process was repeated until each handful of spoons had been buffed.

As I have said the bulk of the buffing operations could be completed on the same 10–12 inch buff. However this was, of course, too large to deal with the insides of the bowls of the spoons, this task was performed on special insiding buffs, those doing the job were called, naturally enough, 'insiders'. Insiding buffs were small circular pieces of leather which were threaded onto the end of a taper-screwed spindle. For table spoons the leather buff was perhaps four inches in diameter and half-an-inch wide; dessert and tea spoons required progressively smaller buffs; and when you got down to salt and mustard spoons the buffs were barely bigger than a button. In fork buffing, again, most of the operations could be completed on the

Sand buffing.

Polishing the inside of a spoon bowl using the 'knee method'. The buffer is seated and upward pressure is applied with the knee.

A typical buffer lass.

larger buff—all except the insides of the prongs. This operation, also performed by the insider, was known as 'graining' and was done on very narrow buffs which, like the larger buffs, were covered with molten resin. Scooping up the sand, the operator held the insides of the fork tines against the edges of the buff at the same time applying sideways pressure.

I soon discovered that there were as many interesting and colourful characters at John Street as in the grinding wheel I had left, and they certainly added to my experience of life and my cutlery education.

Perhaps the most colourful of my immediate colleagues were the Talbot sisters, who announced that they hailed from 'Happy lark—the Park' and certainly they were one of the happiest groups of lasses I ever met. In fact, there were seven girls in their family but only five worked at our place. They had just the one brother, to whom they never referred by his name, Fred, but simply as 'our boy'. What a crowd the Talbots were: they dominated the workshop, filling it with the sound of laughter and singing—and were forever playing tricks which provoked more laughter. They were rather fluent in the use of strong language, but it was a privilege to work with them, for they were amongst the most loyal and friendly people I have ever known, and their work was of a very high quality. They may have been rough diamonds to some eyes, but each in her way, was absolutely genuine and full of character and a warmth which made you glad to be with them. They liked a joke, but could be very serious when it mattered and, working harder than many men, they earned every penny they were paid. Lily, the eldest, was an insider, Cis and Ann were buffers, and Lol and Ruth dolliers. Cis was the boss, the leader; Ann, the youngest was perhaps the prettiest; and Lol, known to everybody as Lollipop, the most exuberant.

Others working in the shop included Iris Pollard and Leah Jowitt, who were handle grinders, and a buffer called Fanny Pemberton. Fanny was a chubby, motherly woman in her fifties, and by contrast with the Talbot sisters she had a quiet sense of humour which, nevertheless, raised many a laugh. I always remember one day when Fanny was rather livelier than usual, it emerged that she had just learned that her son, Jack, had been awarded the Military Medal for performing some act of outstanding bravery whilst serving abroad with the army. The incident served to remind us that the war was still no nearer to an end—and it made me realise that I was fast approaching an age when I could expect to be called up. I think perhaps, also, that Dad heard about Fanny's son with mixed feelings, for at the time we had already heard that my brother Charlie was in a Japanese POW camp.

My closest colleague at John Street for some time was an attractive 16-year-old lass called Olive Wales. She and I worked together on a spindle, both of us glazing solid handles. For some reason we were always falling out and arguing. Looking back, I fancy it might have been something to do with the fact that she was quicker at the job than I was, I always tried to beat her, but she invariably outpaced me. I think it pained me to think that, even at 16, she could earn £5 a week—about £1 more than me.

Sometimes my Upperthorpe pals and I would go to a dance at St Swithin's on the Manor, where 'Tripes' Baker and his three-piece band were the big attraction. We would often see Olive there, she and I would smile at each other and silently agree on a truce as we shared a dance; but once we were back at work the 'daggers drawn' situation would be resumed. In later years we had the sense to forget our teenage rivalry and we became good pals.

I suppose I was a bit impetuous in those days, like any young chap feeling his way in the world and anxious to grow up quickly, as one incident with foreman, Wilf Hattersley, and myself illustrates. We didn't always see eye to eye, Wilf had come to the John Street workshop after being invalided out of the Forces, he taught me a lot of things, including how to cut a serrating wheel and how to serrate, but we often exchanged a few sharp words. There was one famous occasion when we got to blows, Wilf struck the first blow, I hit him back, and the next minute we were rolling about on the floor, with me finishing up on top raining blows at him. It took several of the buffer lasses to separate us.

At John Street I didn't have as much time, as I'd had at Randall Street, to wander off talking to people in the other workshops, but I got to know two of the grinders from next door. One of them, 'Big Reuben' was, for me, a fascinating character, as interesting in his way as Birdy Harrison was, for he, too, had a story to tell. Though born in Sheffield, where he had learned his craft, he had emigrated and become an American citizen. He thrilled me with his reminiscences of his time in the US Cavalry during the Great War;

John Street days, 1942. I am standing with 'Lollipops'.

but it was sobering to hear him tell of the effects of the depression which hit America in the late 1920s and early 1930s. It was as a result of the poverty he'd had to endure during this bleak period that he had chosen to return home. Here he was happier and better off but, as a wide-eyed lad, I couldn't imagine that Sheffield could ever match America in terms of romance.

Romance of another kind was what motivated the other grinder I met at this time. I will refer to him only by the nickname given to him at that time—'Sugars'. He then became Sugars to everybody so I doubt if many people who met him later even knew his real name. It was one of the buffer lasses who told me how he acquired the name Sugars. When he dated one of the girls from the wheel, it caused a stir because everyone knew he was married. Next day the girl was quizzed about what had happened. 'Oh, it was lovely' she said. 'We went to the Lyceum. We sat in the best seats, he bought me a huge box of chocolates, and in the interval he took me into the bar for a drink. Then afterwards we went across to the Adelphi pub, and he plied me with drinks and treated me as if I was very special.' As she lapsed into a starry-eyed silence, one of her mates said 'What tha means, lass, is he was just like a bloody sugar daddy!'

So the name Sugars stuck, and it suited him, for his life was one romantic entanglement after another. He was well known as a lady's man who would 'chase anything in a skirt'. At the time, one of the popular songs of the day included the line 'don't mess with Mister In-between', and when one of the buffer lasses began to sing it, we all knew they had been talking about Sugars and his amorous adventures. Poor chap, he suffered from high blood pressure, which caused his nose to bleed quite a lot but, in the way they had, the buffer lasses turned it into a joke, suggesting that Sugars thought so much about women that his nose bled once a month in sympathy!

His philandering knew no bounds. At one time, for instance, he was having an affair with the landlady of a local pub. The woman's husband had a part-time job, and she and Sugars had an arrangement that if the bedroom curtains were open it meant the coast was clear, but if they were closed then the husband was at home. We used to call this kind of thing 'mankin', and Sugars was a great exponent of the practice.

There was, however, a tragic side to his womanising in that it may have contributed to the suicide of an innocent person—hence the reason I have refrained from giving his real name.

The Happy Teenager

Although the first four years of my working life coincided with what was probably the darkest phase of the war, I have to say that it was a fabulous time for me. I think that the years from the age of 14 to 18 constitute one of the most exciting phases in a man's life, for they span that period during which one leaves boyhood behind and the struggle towards adulthood begins. To me, the world seemed suddenly to fill with enormous hope and potential and I enjoyed a dramatic sense of freedom and opportunity.

After my initial reluctance to enter that black hole called a grinding wheel, I discovered that I could, after all, find some fulfilment in following Dad into the cutlery industry. There was much to absorb and intrigue me in the workshops, and the knowledge and experience I gained was to stand me in good stead in later life. I developed quickly in the work as I had always been an inquisitive lad, eager to learn and interested in acquiring information about production methods and the mysteries of machinery and equipment. Moreover, I always enjoyed the atmosphere of the industry and, for me, the greyness and dampness of the workplace were dispelled by the colourfulness and camaraderie of the people. Those who were my colleagues helped make work a pleasure, a delightful adventure, and I was happy and contented with my lot.

Of course, it wasn't all work. Growing up was a wonderful process, and with my pals I had a great time simply enjoying life. Ours was a robust, boozy and red-blooded existence, with fun and frivolity the keynote as we made sure of getting maximum pleasure for the minimum cost. Yet, if we let our hair down with what now seems astonishing regularity, it wasn't because we had any fears for the future. No doubt we were conscious of the war and we knew that if it continued long enough then our turn to serve in the Armed Forces would come, but we didn't think about the future. We simply lived for the day, no doubt like teenagers of any period in history, ever content to let tomorrow take care of itself.

Naturally, I was conscious that my brother Charlie was serving abroad, and I know now that while I was enjoying my new-found freedom, he was going through hell in a Japanese POW camp where he died of cholera. Perhaps the full knowledge of what he must have endured only came to me as late as 1985 when I took my family to his grave in the Chungkai Cemetery. How beautiful and peaceful that place seemed some forty years after the event; but what suffering Charlie must have endured, especially in his last days. Yet, knowing him, I cannot imagine that he would have wanted me to do other than enjoy my youth. I think he would have been pleased to know I was having so much fun.

Dancing was the main attraction for me and my pals, though in truth it was really boozing that was the big thing, with a little bit of dancing thrown in afterwards. Our favourite haunt was Dey's Ballroom in Pitsmoor. A typical Saturday evening for us began at half-past six when we arrived at the Dove and Rainbow pub in town. At nine we would take the tram to Pitsmoor, make a quick call at Dey's to obtain our admission tickets, and then adjourn to the nearby Bay Horse Inn, returning to the dance hall only when the pub stopped serving beer. If I got too drunk to go home, I would spend the night at a pal's house.

Our drinking and dancing took us all over Sheffield. Apart from the Dove and Rainbow, we used such other city centre pubs as the Stone House and The Bell. Sometimes we might find it more convenient to dance at the City Hall or the Cutlers' Hall, where it was old time dancing in the Hadfield Room on the ground floor and modern dancing in the large banqueting hall above. We went anywhere and everywhere in the quest for fun: St Nathaniels up Crookesmoor Road; St Swithin's on the Manor; St Joseph's at Handsworth; Collinson's in Hanover Street; and the Sacred Heart at Hillsborough. We visited every place where there was dancing at some time or other—and we always knew the most convenient pub! I don't think we really took our dancing seriously, but at least we made the effort to master the basics by attending classes at Constance Grant's!

During those years my weekly wage went up from about 16 shillings to over £4, so I could afford to drink and dance. However, there were times when funds were low, though we were seldom stuck even when we had little or no money left. The cinema was a cheaper form of entertainment than drinking, and if we were really broke we always knew we could get into the Don on West Bar without paying. The toilets at this cinema were outside and it was quite easy to reach them from the street. So, after nipping into the toilet, we took it in turns to stroll into the darkened auditorium—if anyone stopped us we always explained that we had just been to the toilet!

It was a good time, a wonderful time, but we knew it couldn't last for ever. At sixteen I had begun to make a token gesture towards the war effort by becoming an ARP messenger, but as the hostilities continued I knew the day was fast approaching when I would find myself in uniform. Sure enough, one day in the summer of 1943 my call-up papers plopped through the letterbox at Portland Street. I volunteered for the Fleet Air Arm.

It was, I suppose, the end of my youth, the end of my first years of apprenticeship, but I was not dismayed, and I knew that one day I would return. Cutlery had been in my blood from the very outset, but now it was in my heart too. I was confident that once the war was over, I would rejoin Dad and resume my progress towards a successful career in the trade that had been so important to the Housleys for so many generations.

A Very Unable Seaman

Several weeks before my 18th birthday I was instructed to report to the Sheffield United Cricket Pavillion, Cherry Street, for a medical prior to being called-up. A year earlier, by adding a year to his age, my best pal Bob Price, who was one day older than me, had volunteered for the Fleet Air Arm as an Air Mechanic. Our friendship goes back to schooldays and still remains.

I wanted to emulate him but my parents threatened to inform the authorities if I did. In retrospect this was quite understandable, my parents were thinking of Charlie's fate.

After the medical I was asked which service I preferred and immediately plumped for the Fleet Air Arm. On being asked if I would like to become a Telegraphist Air Gunner I willingly accepted. My call-up papers and railway warrant arrived shortly after my 18th birthday with instructions to report to *HMS Royal Arthur*, Skegness, on 5th October 1943.

The night before my departure I was given a rousing send off at a party which took place in the best room, (we usually used the tap room) of the Victoria Hotel, Addy Street, a beer-only house. With drinks coming from all directions, even the landlord sent them in, I'm afraid I over-imbibed.

Next morning suffering from the mother of all hangovers I boarded the train at Victoria Station and spent most of the journey lying down on the bench-seat of the ancient, corridorless carriage. On arrival at Skegness we learned that *HMS Royal Arthur* was none other than Butlins Holiday Camp—which Lord Haw Haw (the German propaganda broadcaster), claimed to have sunk on several occasions! At *Royal Arthur* we lived in chalets and slept in the former holiday camp's beds, despite being issued with hammocks, which, after several abortive attempts, we learned to get in and out of.

The first two days were taken up with numerous injections, the issue of kit and a general induction into the navy and I soon met the rest of my fellow

Butlins Skegness, 1943, HMS Royal Arthur. *I am 2nd left on the 4th row.*

HMS St Vincent, *Gosport, a training establishment for Fleet Air Arm recruits (1943). I am on the extreme left of the 4th row.*

recruits to the 60th TAG course. They came from all walks of life and from all parts of the UK, amongst them were several university graduates. Our five weeks at *Royal Arthur* were spent square bashing, running, swimming, assault course training and generally getting fit. Some of my companions had the additional task which was to learn Sheffield-speak. My accent was so broad then that an interpreter was often needed.

We were taught the rudiments of seamanship, unarmed combat and weaponry. Our drill instructor, Petty Officer Dusty Rhodes, was a foul-mouthed bully who thoroughly enjoyed tyrannising his young charges. I believe the object of this treatment was to instil discipline and immediate response to all commands. In this he succeeded for we all feared him.

Our next 'ship' was *HMS St Vincent*, an old training barracks in Gosport where TAGs and observers were given initial schooling then exams prior to being sent for further training. Each morning we paraded on the barrack square and, afterwards, marched to a Royal Marines' Band—a stirring experience which made the blood tingle. The drum major, a dashing figure, flourished and twirled with great panache, a long, ornate, regimental baton mounted with a silver dome. His party piece, which never failed, was to fling the baton high in the air as we approached the huge, brick-built, domed, entrance archway then, without losing step, and with nonchalant ease, he caught it on the other side as we passed through!

At *St Vincent* we were beginning to feel like real sailors. It was here where we were made to climb the rope rigging of an enormously high mast. Near the top was a platfrom, where the rope rigging turned outwards from the mast at an angle of 45 degrees to the ground about a hundred feet below. With our backs facing the ground we scrambled, almost upside down, onto the platform feeling greatly relieved at our success. Above the platform the mast continued without the rope rigging. Some daredevils (myself not included) wrapped their arms and legs around the mast and hauled themselves up to the top where they stood on the 'button' at the very pinnacle.

Intensive training in Morse code, wireless telegraphy, flag signal recognition, radio theory, and small weapons ensued. Words like resistance, inductance, ohm, condenser, resonance, impedance, frequency, plus many others, became part of our everyday vocabulary. This was all very different from tables, desserts, palettes and scrapers, which were some of the different types of knife blades I was used to speaking of, but I was certainly glad to be in the fresh air, away from the dust and fumes of the cutlers' workshop.

Whilst at Gosport we experienced several air raids, aimed mainly at nearby Portsmouth. In the event of air raids we had each been allocated places of duty, mine was to help to man an ancient, manually-operated turntable fire-ladder. There was wishful talk of 'rescuing' some Wrens from their nearby dormitories but it never came to anything! The Portsmouth searchlight and anti-aircraft barrage was a sight to behold. On one occasion, I recall, one of our own aircraft was caught in the searchlights and, due to its lateness in firing the recognition flare, came under heavy fire. Fortunately, it survived.

Round about Christmas we received 7-days leave. Even though I had only been away for three months it was great to see my parents, brother and friends again. I purposely visited the workshop on Monday, where my former workmates, buffer lasses and cutlers, made a great fuss of me and then followed a bit of a Saint Monday knees up in The Ship in John Street, with lots of singing and drinking. Whilst on leave I bumped into the vicar of our local church, Sid Tredinick, who insisted that I attend the Sunday service. I blushed to the roots when the congregation sang the hymn containing the words, 'For those in peril on the sea' at the time the only ship I had been on was the Gosport ferry, but the kindly old man meant well. Lots of dancing, drinking and partying took place in the short time available but, in what seemed no time at all, it was time to return to Gosport.

In January 1944 we were posted to the Number One Naval Air Gunnery School, at the Royal Canadian Air Force Station, Yarmouth, Nova Scotia. After a brief stay in Townhill transit camp, Dunfermline, where we were issued with our tropical kit, including pith helmet, we departed for Liverpool and embarked on the Royal Mail Ship *Andes*, a luxury cruise liner.

The crossing of the North Atlantic, my first sea voyage, was accompanied by gale force 10 winds, enormously high seas and seasickness but, after about three days, I found my sea legs. The *Andes*, like similar, fast passenger liners converted to troop-carrying duties during the war, sailed unaccompanied, relying on her speed to evade submarines. During the crossing there was a warning of submarines in the area on our original course so we diverted towards Iceland to avoid them. It was an uncomfortable experience when the alarm sounded calling the crew to action stations, we passengers, down in the bowels of the ship below the waterline, had to don lifebelts and just hang around doing nothing but wait and listen.

Our early morning arrival in Halifax, Nova Scotia, was greeted by clear skies, a bitterly cold wind and sub-zero temperatures. Once ashore we entrained for Moncton, New Brunswick, the home of a transit camp where RAF and naval airmen stayed for a few days prior to departure for their allotted training establishment in the USA or Canada. The main thing I remember of Moncton is the River Miramichi where, twice a day, a great tidal bore, several feet high, sweeps up river. This tidal wave originates in the Bay of Fundy where tides of seventy feet are not uncommon.

On arrival at East Camp we were allowed a couple of days to settle in, during which time we were issued with flying gear, then our training began in earnest. After a pre-breakfast run through Yarmouth town we received daily sessions of Morse code and, in addition to the usual buzzers and headphones, we did visual work using Aldis lamps. We also received more schooling in the workings and use of radio transmitter–receivers and weapons training. Sports, athletics and games were also prominent and we became very fit.

At last came our first flight, in an Anson Mark II training aircraft. Unfortunately, my own flying training, and life as a Telegraphist Air Gunner, was to be short lived. At the age of five, shortly after starting school, whilst chasing about, I was involved in a heavy collision with another child during playtime and I suffered a badly broken nose. Instead of sending me to hospital, the Headmistress, Miss Fanny Dunk, laid me on the floor beneath a large table she used as a desk. A large iron key was put down the back of my neck which, I believe, was supposed to stop the bleeding. Consequently, my broken nose was never treated. Because of the bruising and swelling my parents never realised at the time the extent of the injury and, as a result, for the next fifteen years I could only breathe through my mouth.

Shortly after our first flight we were given further medical examinations by RCAF doctors. During my medical my nose, which was slightly bruised after receiving a knock playing football, came in for close inspection and I was told that I would not be allowed to fly again until the blocked up air passages, had been dealt with. This meant a return to England on the liner *Ille de France*, I arrived in May 1944. The main base for all Fleet Air Arm personnel was at Lee-on-Solent and on the train journey there I saw mile after mile of country lanes and hedgerows lined with tanks, trucks and every conceivable army vehicle, all standing by for the imminent D-Day landings of June 6th 1944.

My papers had preceded me from Canada but I was informed that it could take several months before an appointment to have my nose fixed could be arranged. By then there was a strong possibility that further recruitment of TAGs would have ceased. It had, therefore, been decided to transfer me from the Fleet Air Arm to the Royal Navy for training as a seaman. Shortly afterwards, I reported to *HMS Ganges*, Shotley, near Ipswich, another training barracks, where, instead of a Naval Airman first class, I became an Ordinary Seaman.

After the training, which took about three months to complete, I was posted to *HMS Pembroke*, Chatham Barracks (another 'ship' often sunk by Lord Haw Haw) there to await an operation on my nose before being posted to a real ship. I was accommodated in the nearby Collingwood Camp, run as an independent unit to the main barracks and was told to report to the galley.

With the exception of six seamen who, amongst other things undertook any heavy lifting, the galley was staffed entirely by Wrens, working in two watches. As an unattached matelot, and one of six seamen amongst forty

Wrens, it felt like winning the pools. We certainly made the most of it, getting up to all kinds of pranks, despite the constant beady eyes of 'Hatchet Face' the Chief Petty Officer Wren in charge.

On one occasion, whilst hosing down the preparation benches, a Wren turned the hose on a seaman who immediately lifted her up and deposited her, screaming and kicking, into a large tub of cold water. She went berserk and, picking up a cleaver, chased him out of the galley and round the camp—much to the amusement and raucous encouragement of all onlookers. On another occasion the Wrens, who had been parading on the barrack square, were being inspected by a senior officer. Suddenly, a black cat, its tail sheathed in a condom courtesy of the galley seamen, casually sauntered past them! There was an official investigation into that particular prank but, although everyone was confined to barracks for a week, the culprits were never found.

My particular girlfriend was a Wren called Mary Abrahams, she came from the North East, Sunderland I think. We often went to the pictures and for walks along the headland near Rochester together. I lost touch after being posted and have often wondered what happened to her.

The officer commanding East Camp was Commander Stubbs, an old buffer of World War One vintage who would have made a great candidate for Dad's Army. Although he dined in the Officers' Mess, he always knew when fish and chips were on the menu for the ratings, and he invariably came to one of us for a piece of fresh fish—allegedly for his invalid wife. We had no guilty conscience in complying with his request because we were always issued with rations for everyone on the camp's strength. This was despite the fact that each evening, before dinner had been served, dozens, if not hundreds, went ashore or up to the Smoke (London) for the night. This always resulted in large amounts of cooked food being thrown away, a shocking state of affairs when one considered the perils undertaken to provide it. Apart from that, Old Stubbsey never refused us a weekend pass whenever we needed one. A favourite saying in the navy was, 'If you can't beat a racket, join it', and who were we to argue with tradition?

Towards the end of 1944, I received a letter from Little Joe, one of our former group who, because of a lifelong physical disability was unfit for any branch of the armed forces. Joe's letter told of his forthcoming shotgun wedding and he asked if I would be his best man.

It transpired that he was to marry Mary, one of a group of three young ladies we had met at a Friday night hop at the Darnall Public hall a few months before my call-up. This had been a memorable night because when, as arranged, we met them the following Sunday morning for a hike in the country, Audrey, a real good looker, the one Little Joe had walked home the previous Friday, had turned up with an enormous black eye. This had been handed to her by her irate father for coming home so late and for having the smell of alcohol on her breath—a summary punishment, she was also banned from going to any more dances. She had only managed to get out that morning, because her dad was working.

On the strength of being best man at a wedding I was able to wangle a 'Friday while' pass from old Stubbsey. To mark the event I decided to buy my first tiddly suit. Naval ratings received 3d per day (1.25p) clothing allowance, officially designated as Kit Upkeep Allowance. We usually bought our clothing from Slops, the naval term for the stores, where all standard items from handkerchiefs to full suits could be purchased at remarkably low prices.

However, if you wanted something smarter, made from a better cloth with extra wide bell bottoms and a very tight waistline, you visited a naval tailor in Chatham Town for a made-to-measure suit. This was kept as best and known as a tiddly suit, everyone had one. My old aunt Fanny always said that I had a figure like a Henderson's Relish bottle, straight up and down, she was of course right and a tiddly suit proved to be a waste of money in my case.

I cannot recall anything about the wedding ceremony itself but Joe's stag night the previous evening had been quite eventful. I know we started off in the city centre visiting all our favourite pubs but, sometime after midnight, the groom-to-be almost got arrested for being drunk and disorderly in Pitsmoor Road. He was only singing some of his favourite songs, but when I recall his foghorn of a voice and total inability to sing in tune, there could have been slight grounds for complaint!

Big Harry, who had a pronounced stutter when excited, fancied himself as a bit of an advocate. After much pleading and several heartbreaking stories about Little Joe's painful upbringing, coupled with the fact that he was losing his freedom anyway, he finally persuaded the PC, who had appeared out of the blackout from nowhere, to live and let live. We were told to be on our way but further singing was definitely out.

The wedding reception was held at the home of the bride, all the neighbours having chipped in a few ration coupons to enable a good spread to be provided. Her father and two brothers, all miners, were in charge of the drinks. Dad was also a virtuoso on the melodeon so the party was soon going with a swing.

One of the bridesmaids, Irene, was the third of the trio we had met at the Darnall Public Hall the previous year, we often corresponded and met each other when I was on leave, but there was nothing serious. Irene was a nurse and had to be on duty at 6am the following morning.

The bride's home was quite small, downstairs consisting of a dining kitchen and a front parlour. Food and drink was being served in the kitchen and people were milling around consuming it. To increase the seating capacity a plank had been placed across two tall circular stools, it overhung at both ends. Harry, one of the bride's brothers, with a pint in one hand and a large plate of food in the other, was seated right at one end next to the open door leading into the kitchen—he was minding his own business. A couple were sitting on the other end in deep conversation, they seemed oblivious to anyone else in the room.

With unbelievable timing, the couple stood up simultaneously. Down went the end of the plank Harry was sitting on, his beer and plate of food shot up into the air, he crashed into the open door which reciprocated by crashing down on top of Harry! This all happened in the blink of an eye. It could not have been bettered by the Keystone Cops after weeks of rehearsing and fifty takes. Mum came dashing into the room to see what was happening whilst Harry kept repeating 'I never moved, I never moved, honestly Mum, I never moved'.

'What about the door' cried mum.

'It's not our bloody door' consoled Dad, whose melodeon playing had temporarily ceased, 'It belongs t'council. They can come and fix it on Monday.'

With that the door was carted into the backyard and the party continued.

By this time, what with all the food and drink of the past few days, I was beginning to wish that I had not held my breath and pulled my stomach in whilst being measured for my tiddly suit. I could hardly move and was most uncomfortable. After removing my sailors collar and black silk, it took two men to pull off the skin-tight top whilst I leaned forward with arms above my head—what a relief.

Shortly after midnight Irene decided that it was time for her to catch a few hours sleep before she had to go on duty. As I walked her home, it was a balmy night with no need to replace my unifrom top, we began to hear the distant sound of aircraft engines. Suddenly the air raid sirens began to scream their alarming and undulating wails. As the noise grew nearer I realised they were V1 flying bombs, known as Doodle Bugs, the first of Hitler's secret weapons. In the south of England, where I was stationed, they were an almost daily and nightly occurrence. Doodle Bugs were powered by a new type of engine whose sound was totally different and much noisier than any previous airborne sound, once heard it was unmistakable. They could out-speed any of our piston-engined aircraft and the newly invented jet-engined aircraft were just being introduced in very small numbers.

I told Irene that she only needed to worry should the noise suddenly stop, for it was then that the missile plunged from the sky to wreak its fearful and random destruction. I understand that night was the one and only time during the whole of the war that Doodle Bugs flew over Sheffield. I believe they landed on the moors somewhere east of Stockport, but cannot be certain.

After a pleasant interlude saying goodnight and promising to write more often, I wended my way back to the wedding party where the rest of my uniform still remained. On arrival I soon discovered that Doodle Bugs were not the only flyers out that night, my return had been preceded by a visit from the Flying Squad. Apparently some long-standing feud between the families of the bride's mum and dad had erupted resulting in a brawl, with not only fists but bottles flying. The mirror above the sideboard was smashed—perhaps an omen of seven years bad luck for someone?

The bride's mum had dialled 999 from the nearest telephone kiosk, hence the visit from the boys in blue. By the time I arrived all was quiet and everyone the best of friends again. No one believed me when I told them that the reason for the air raid warning was Doodle Bugs, at least not until they saw the next day's headlines in the *Star* 'Doodle Bugs Over Sheffield'. A fitting climax to my first experience of being best man at a wedding.

Eventually, an appointment was made for me to attend the famous East Grinstead Cottage Hospital, Sussex, home of the Guinea Pig Club. It was here that Sir Archibald McIndoe and his fellow surgeons performed minor miracles of surgery on the horrendously burned airmen who had been shot down in flames. Archie himself, in his operating gown and white wellies, examined my nose and told me I would be sent for when a bed became available.

Towards the end of 1944, I was admitted to the hospital, where the King's personal ENT specialist, Sir George Scott-Browne, performed the first of three operations on my nose. Afterwards long rubber tubes, which seemed to go down into my throat, were inserted into my nostrils to prevent the air passages from closing up again whilst they healed. When the tubes were removed, a week or two later, an electrically driven sucker, a bit like a miniature vacuum cleaner, was used to remove any blood and puss. The ability to breathe freely through my nose, for the first time since childhood, was a most welcome experience.

The second operation, a refracture, was to straighten my nose which was crooked. After this my whole nose was placed in plaster. Finally, a bone graft operation was performed, using bone taken from my hip, this was to replace that removed during the first operation.

Afterwards I had a beautiful looking nose. A marine commando, with whom I palled up and who had undergone similar treatment, had a much larger piece of bone grafted inside his nose and the result was a large, hooked, Roman nose. Since then, however, mine has settled leaving me with what looks like a professional boxer's nose, whereas I suppose the marine, whom I haven't seen since, has probably now got a perfect aquiline hooter! Between operations we were accommodated in The Annexe, a nearby stately country home, where the food and accommodation were superb. I was still at East Grinstead when the war in Europe ended in May 1945 and the celebrations, which continued for several days and nights, were most memorable.

The majority of patients at East Grinstead were badly burned RAF airmen, many of them Battle of Britain pilots. With just a broken nose, and that the result of a childhood accident, I felt like an impostor. Seeing young men without eyelids, lips, noses and ears, their badly burned hands mutilated almost beyond recognition, made me realise more than ever what a great debt the nation owed to these courageous airmen. Experiencing the tremendous spirit of cheerfulness and the atmosphere of *bonhomie* that existed between the Guinea Pigs was something I shall never forget.

One such patient was Richard Pape, author of *Boldness Be My Friend*, an account of his capture after being shot down over Berlin. This tough Yorkshire airman made several attempts to escape but was always being recaptured, once on the very night he was due to be taken off by a British submarine. Despite being tortured by the Gestapo, he eventually made it to neutral Sweden. On his return to flying duties he crashed, was badly disfigured, and, after unsatisfactory treatment at other hospitals, was finally taken to East Grinstead. His words, reproduced below, describe far better than I ever could the spirit he found there:

> It turned out that in addition to plastic repairs, I also received the best cures for my mental condition. I met at East Grinstead the finest bunch of Royal Air Force men I have ever encountered; the grandest body of men that I am ever likely to live among. Man is capable of many expressions of courage, but none, to my mind, compares with the magnificent spirit which emanated from East Grinstead.
>
> Richard Pape, author of *Boldness be my Friend*

Amen to that.

The Guinea Pig Club members, and with them all service patients of East Grinstead Cottage Hospital, were the most favoured group of servicemen to benefit from the benevolence of actors, actresses, producers, directors and management from London's West End theatres. There were open invitations, free of charge, to most shows. All we had to do was see the hospital's Welfare Officer and, usually for a group of four, a trip was arranged, with free transport, the best seats, invitations back stage and free drinks.

Amongst the patients was a loveable, little cockney ragamuffin, Billy Mundy, aged, at a guess, about twelve. My understanding, and I trust that I am not doing them any injustice, is that Billy and three other lads were residents of a corrective training establishment for unruly boys. The four had been out walking when one of them saw a shiny object in a field. Billy reached it first and, as he picked it up, it exploded. It was a phosphorous incendiary bomb, they cannot be put out once ignited. All four pals were badly burned, Billy the most seriously, with horrendous burns mainly to his body and hands, fortunately, much of his face escaped. When I first met him he had become the pet of the hospital on account of his great courage and cheerfulness during his many operations, and in the painful recovery periods afterwards. As so much of his body had been burned, there was very little area left from where skin for grafts could be taken. Despite his suffering, his cockney impudence and the indomitable spirit in his small body shone out like a beacon.

When his treatment permitted we sometimes took him with us up to London to see a show, and one I particularly recall, was a revue at the London Palladium called 'Happy and Glorious'. The star of the show was

Sir Archie McIndoe, the famous wartime surgeon, entertaining some of his 'guinea pig' airmen.

Tommy Trinder, one of Billy's heroes, who did a great job entertaining the troops in all theatres of war. In Tommy's dressing room after the show, Billy was asking all sorts of questions and getting comical answers received by great howls of laughter, especially from Billy. We had been given drinks but, as there was nothing suitable for Billy to drink, Tommy said to him 'I'll tell you what Billy, you can choose anything on my dressing table', which was crowded with momentos, 'as a present to take back to East Grinstead.' After a good look at everything Billy chose a silver model aeroplane, when you turned the propeller, the cockpit flew open and a flame appeared. It was an unusual cigarette lighter made by an air fitter and given to Tommy whilst entertaining the troops in North Africa. On the train journey back to East Grinstead no one was allowed to touch his precious gift. Subsequently, he fell asleep clutching it to his chest with his badly burned and shrivelled hands.

On another occasion, this time without Billy, we saw the play *Tomorrow the World* featuring the lovely Elizabeth Allen. Afterwards, we were invited to her flat for supper, when I told her that before the war, on an outing organised by my Sunday School, I had thoroughly enjoyed seeing the film *Oliver Twist* in which she starred, she laughed and told me I made her feel ancient.

During the return journey, in the blacked out compartment, conversation became philosophical and plans for the better world we hoped to help create after the war featured in the discussion. Matthew, a very badly burned young airman, whose right hand had been amputated and who had been blinded, suddenly, in the most plaintive voice, began to sing the song, 'Just to see my mother smile again'—a moment I'll never forget.

On being discharged from East Grinstead I was given two weeks leave. I then returned to Chatham Barracks and, after being kept hanging around for yet a few more months, I was finally posted to a real ship. This was towards the end of 1945, the war having ended a few months earlier. I did not have much of a war record—but then I had no choice in the matter.

HMS Rajah, one of the so-called banana boats, had been mass produced in the USA by a shipbuilder named Kaiser. He had taken the design of a merchant ship, used before the war for transporting bananas from the Caribbean to various parts of the world, and adapted it for use as a small aircraft carrier. She had a top speed of around 16 knots, about half that of the fast fleet carriers.

These ships were known as Escort Carriers and fulfilled many roles such as convoy protection, air cover for other warships, torpedo and bomb attacks on enemy shipping and shore installations, and cover for assault ships during landings on enemy beaches. They were also used for the delivery of replacement aircraft, lost in battle or by accident, to the much larger, mainstream, fleet carriers.

When I joined the *Rajah* she was being used as a troopship. All aircraft and ancillary equipment had been removed and the hangars fitted with bunks. Our task was to ferry young, recently trained servicemen to the Far East and various ports en route. We then brought back the veterans who had served in many theatres of war during the preceding years. Our ports of call after leaving Chatham were Southampton, where we picked up young troops from the three services, then across the Bay of Biscay to Gibraltar, through the Mediterranean to Malta then Port Said. Sailing through the Suez canal was a strange experience, huge ships seemingly floating across the desert. On one occasion we stayed overnight in the Great Bitter Lakes. Opposite to where we lay, three captured Italian Battleships were berthed. After the ship had anchored the instruction, 'Hands to bathing stations,' was piped over the Tannoy System. This was the signal for hundreds of us to dive, jump or get pushed over the side for a refreshing swim in extremely salty water.

At the far end of the canal is Port Suez at the head of the beautiful Red Sea. Dolphins and porpoises criss-crossed at speed in front of the ship's bows. Flying fish abounded and we saw the occasional school of whales. Towards the bottom end of the Red Sea lies Aden, another of our ports of call, with a backdrop of towering rocks, no vegetation and intense heat—few of us went ashore. Here, young, naked boys would dive for coins thrown from the flight

HMS Rajah *a wartime escort carrier, one of many produced in the USA for Allied navies.*

deck high above the sea. They could remain underwater for surprisingly long periods of time and resurfaced with the coins stored in their mouths. The bum-boats were another feature of Aden. Arab traders with all kinds of wares would barter a price, perhaps for a watch, rug, or leather bag, which was then tied to a rope and hauled up by the buyer.

After passing through the Sea of Aden we crossed the Indian Ocean to Colombo in Ceylon (now Sri Lanka). We then steamed on through the Straits of Malacca, with the jungles of Malaysia and Sumatra rising on either side, to Singapore, a magnificent natural harbour and, finally, up through the South China Seas to our last port of call Hong Kong.

During the outward journey, with short stays for refuelling and victualling, we disembarked the young servicemen. They were to be replacements for the troops already out there, some of whom had not seen the UK for years. For the return journey we began taking on smiling veterans, happy to be on the way back to Blighty at last. The round trip took, approximately, three months to complete.

With the war over and plenty of room on the flight deck for sunbathing, or sports, such as deck hockey and deck football, played with a canvas ball

On the flight deck of the Rajah *when she was anchored off Aden.*

made up by the sailmaker, one could wish for nothing better. People today are paying thousands of pounds for similar cruises.

On my third and last trip the *Rajah's* engines broke down in the Indian Ocean and we drifted for approximately 24 hours. The engines were, eventually, restarted and we limped into Colombo for temporary repairs which took about three weeks to complete. Whilst in Ceylon we swam regularly in the sea at the nearby, famous, Mount Lavinia beach where huge rollers crashed in from the ocean. On one occasion I, along with some shipmates, swam out to some rocks about half a mile offshore. This had been quite easy but the return journey, swimming against a strong offshore current, was most difficult and not attempted again.

Several local fishermen lived, with their families, beside the beach in crude, palm-thatched huts. The sailing craft they used were primitive, but highly efficient, outrigger canoes which could cover long distances at surprising speed with their single sail.

Trips to Kandy, the ancient capital of Ceylon and home of the Sacred Temple of the Tooth and an enormous reclining figure of Buddha, known as the Lying Buddha, were arranged. Visits to tea and rubber plantations were included and, also, to the famous botanical gardens where, amongst many other interesting tropical flora, we saw large carnivorous plants which obtained their nutrients from birds and small mammals which they ensnared. (They were apparently from the same family as the Venus Fly Trap we know here.) By the time we arrived back on board they had become man-eating plants!

With our engines finally repaired, we left Colombo for England. The start of my 21st birthday found me on duty for the middle watch, (midnight to 4 am) the first two hours were spent on lookout high in the crows nest, above the island bridge which is the nerve centre of an aircraft carrier. The night was calm and perfectly clear with a myriad of brightly shining stars, best appreciated at sea in the tropics. Gazing at those twinkling stars, despite my youth and naivety, in a few moments of insight, or was it intuition, I realised that, tiny speck though the world may be in the enormous galaxies, with myself an even smaller speck in relation to the world, anything was achievable, the world belonged to the young. At twenty-one, with the return to civilian life just a few months away, a wonderful future beckoned. Those thoughts have always remained with me and, by and large, proved true.

I thoroughly enjoyed my time in the Royal Navy, especially the comparatively short time I spent at sea. I enjoyed great companionship, lots of laughs and getting into scrapes. The months from April to July 1947 found me, along with many of my former shipmates, in the Royal Navy Barracks Chatham impatiently awaiting demobilisation. The *Rajah* was a lease–lend ship, loaned by the USA to the Royal Navy for the duration, and returned to a Naval base in Norfolk, Virginia, early in 1947. We, as her crew, then returned to our home port of Chatham where, with seemingly nothing to do, we failed to understand why we should not be demobilised straight away. As always, bureaucracy had taken over, and we were kept hanging around for several months before, eventually, being allowed to return to civvy street in July 1947.

Whilst awaiting release from the forces, talk had often turned to what we hoped to achieve once back in civvy street. I intended to continue my career in cutlery and distinctly recall saying that within one year of demob I hoped to be earning ten pounds a week. At the time this was thought to be riches beyond our wildest dreams and I was ridiculed for having such unattainable ambitions. Our pay at the time, after almost four years service, was not much more than two pounds per week.

In my uniform at the age of 19.

Return
to Work

When I first started working for my father he employed about ten
people at the grinding wheel. Later, some time in 1942, in addition to
the grinding wheel, he set up a cutlers and buffing workshop at a nearby
factory in John Street thus getting closer to becoming a fully fledged cutlery
manufacturer.

During my four years absence from the cutlery industry, the expansion my
father started just before I was called-up continued. This was due not only
to a plentiful supply of work but also to some help from a winning long-odds
bet on the 'spring double'. For the uninitiated two major horse races take
place in the early spring of each year. The Lincolnshire Handicap heralded
the start of the flat racing season, followed, a week later, by the Grand
National which just about concluded the National Hunt programme.
Months before these races took place bookies offered long odds on all horses
entered, many of which never ran. If, however, you were extremely lucky
and picked the winners of both races, coupling them in a spring double, a
popular gamble in those days, you could hit the jackpot. A £10 double on
two horses whose long odds were both 50-1 would win £25,500—untold
wealth in the 1940s.

During the war, many grinders and other cutlery workers had left the
industry for better paid and less demanding jobs. Others had been called up
and, having lived in the fresh air or worked in a modern factory, many of
them never returned to the dirty, cold and damp grinding wheel or buffing
shop—who can blame them? Pay for cutlery workers had always been poor
and continued to be so, even though minimum rates of pay were
implemented by the Cutlery Wages Council, one of dozens of similar
government departments set up many years earlier. They covered much of
industry and commerce, and were intended to prevent unscrupulous
employers from exploiting the workforce. The worst firms were known as
bread and fat shops, meaning that anyone who worked there received such

poor wages that their families had to live on bread and dripping (fat). Some were also known as 'nobbing 'oles'; which indicated that the boss was also a slave driver.

Whole chapters could be written on the pros and cons of how, in a world famous industry, this situation should exist, I'll restrict myself to stating that, in my opinion, and certainly in my lifetime, cutlery had almost always been underpriced. During the war, and for several years afterwards, prices were controlled by the government, materials were in extremely short supply and were rationed. A good many of the manufacturing processes were put out to sub-contractors (Little Mesters), who, by the time they had paid their expenses, earned little more than those employed directly.

Most of the manufacturers were small family-owned businesses, and, after price controls were lifted, they were so afraid of losing business that they allowed buyers to dictate prices. The post-war labour shortages led to the rapid development of new machines by engineering companies who specialised in supplying the cutlery industry, Walters and Dobson Limited, and Morgan Fairest Limited are two companies that spring to mind. Machines had existed before then but not many firms installed them preferring to rely on the cheap, skilled labour force readily available. No cutlery machine has yet been invented that can equal the dexterity of a skilled craftsman's hand.

My father, instead of giving all his winnings back to the bookmaker as most gamblers do, wisely purchased several of these machines, installing them in four workshops he now rented at Enterprise Works, at the corner of St Mary's Road and Shoreham Street. It was to here that I returned just a few days after being demobilised.

Although my father's invoices still modestly proclaimed H. Housley, Grinder he had, in fact, become a fully fledged manufacturer. Included in his new equipment were two knife grinding machines newly developed by Walters and Dobson, a company long since closed down. It speaks volumes for the skill involved in the design and durability of these machines, purchased in 1945, that these two selfsame machines are still in daily use in 1998. They were bought many years ago by a sub-contract grinder called Jack Wild and are installed at his workshop on the outskirts of Sheffield.

Much has been written, and spoken, about the alleged failure of Sheffield cutlery manufacturers to invest in new plant and equipment after World War II. I am not sure that this criticism is justified, as several Sheffield engineering companies were working flat out for several years after the war supplying and developing machinery exclusively for cutlery manufacture. Two firms have already been mentioned, others included H. Slater and Sons Limited, and E.E. Laycock and Sons Limited.

A Walters & Dobson knife grinding machine.

Les Ellis at work on a Laycock felting machine from which the safety guards have been removed.

Some of the larger cutlery companies were developing and building their own specialised machinery and, at the same time, newly designed cutlery manufacturing equipment was being imported from the United States, Germany and Italy.

The fact that the Sheffield Cutlery and Silverware industry is but a tiny shadow of its former self is indisputable, but the reasons for this are many and varied and it will be left to future historians to explain the decline and fall of such vast tracts of British Industry during the past fifty years.

It was at Enterprise Works which, I believe, originally belonged to J.G. Graves, the famous Sheffield businessman and benefactor, that I first met 'Tiger'—although a less tigerish man cannot be imagined. His real name was Johnny Booth and I never did find out how he became known as Tiger, he lived with his elderly father in a back-to-back house in Boston Street.

A scarecrow might have been ashamed to wear Tiger's greasy, stained working clothes, which fitted only where they touched him. The collarless, striped, flannelette shirt he wore, winter and summer, emphasised his long, scrawny neck and huge Adams apple, which, together with his sallow complexion and old cloth cap, made him look much older than a man in his late forties. His baggy trousers, held up by a pair of old army braces with a loop sticking out at either side where buttons were missing, plus the inevitable fag end he always seemed to be smoking, completed his workday wardrobe. His large hands always seemed to be covered in the black bobbing grease which was used on the felt bobs.

Appearances count for so little and in Tiger's case concealed a naturally comical and gentle character, in the style of Stan Laurel whom he somewhat resembled in both appearance and mannerisms. 'Did tha know I'm Archie Webster's chief maggot trainer?' he asked me one morning. Archie was an angler pal of my father's who bred his own maggots and was no mean fisherman. 'There's a big match this weekend and ah've been up all neet exercising his latest hatch of maggots. Did tha know that Archie's got some o' t' best duty stallion bluebottles in Yorkshire? He only breeds pure liver maggots from pedigree stock an ah've got 'em trained to peak condition. They're so aggressive after being fed wi' my secret recipe, once they're on t'hook an in't watter they'll grab fish wit' throat an' never let go 'til they're in't net. Apart from that,' he went on 'they look so good ah could eight 'em missen in a sanwidge.' This was typical of Tiger's conversation, you could never tell whether he was serious or not.

Although it was assumed that he was a confirmed bachelor, his main interests in life being drinking, smoking, backing horses and greyhounds, and supporting Sheffield Wednesday, there had been some talk of a mysterious lady friend. This intrigued the buffer lasses, who all tended to mother him on account of his lack of personal care and the fact that he was so thin.

My father, on the left, fishing on the River Witham.

One morning, Fanny Pemberton, a short, plump, buffer lass who always wore the traditional clothes of her trade—white cover-all, known as a buffbrat, red scarf round her head, and brown paper round her legs—said to Tiger, 'How's tha girl friend love?'

'Tha's got to be careful where wimmin are concerned. Look what happened to Adelaide last week.' Tiger responded.

'Is that what they call 'er, your lady friend?'

'No, it's mi next door neighbour's daughter.'

'What happened to her?'

'It were like this. She brought her boyfriend 'ome one night last week. It had snowed most o't day and was bitterly cold outside. Her Mum and Dad welcomed him in and gave him a cup o' tea and a biscuit. Time passed and the lad showed no sign of leaving until, at last, her Dad said it was getting late and they all had to be up early for work next morning. With that the lad got up and went to the door. Adelaide put her coat on and followed him saying she was just going to say goodnight and wouldn't be long. Shortly afterwards Mum and Dad went upstairs to bed. Once undressed Dad had a peek through the curtains and quickly turned to his wife, who by now was in bed, and said 'Ay up Gladys, that lad's peed in't snow!'

'Well, he's got to relieve hissen' she replied.

'Aye, I know that, but he's written our Adelaide's name in't snow wi' his pee!'

'Well, I shun't wurry about that. Come to bed, he's in love with 'er.'

'Ah, tha may be reight' moaned Dad, 'but it's in our Adelaide's handwriting!'

With that everyone, myself included, erupted into howls of laughter realising that, although he had looked so serious when telling the tale, it was just another one of Tiger's stories. I've heard the story many times since, and believe Les Dawson once used it on TV. No doubt it was an old chestnut when I first heard it from Tiger, but I never laughed so much as when he told it.

My return to work coincided with a post-war boom in the Sheffield cutlery industry. The main problems being faced were the lack of raw materials and skilled labour. I was given a roving commission which included working in the knife grinding shop which was on the ground floor. Tiger, who performed the next operation, worked on the floor above and we were constantly in contact and became good mates.

A Walters & Dobson multi-polishing machine.

St Mary's Road

The main entrance to Enterprise Works was through a large archway, typical of the architecture of old factories. The cobblestoned floor beneath the archway had doors leading off on either side to different workshops. Once through the archway a small yard opened up, revealing more workshops and some steel steps, with tubular steel handrails, leading to the upper floors. It was at the rear of the yard, after passing underneath an overhead covered walkway which connected some upper storey workshops, that my father's rented workshops were located.

Enterprise Works at the corner of Shoreham Street and St Mary's Road.

Ken Croft, who inherited his father Wilf's blade hardening business.

On the ground floor was a small lean-to room which housed the hardening and tempering plant where another ex-sailor nicknamed Scouse held sway. The equipment he used was quite unsophisticated. It consisted of a fan-assisted gas burner which heated, up to temperatures of approximately 1,100 degrees centigrade, a deep cast-steel pot containing molten lead, this gave off a dull red glow when it reached the required temperature, monitored by a pyrometer, for hardening. Everything was housed in a thick steel cabinet, the top half of which was partly cut away at the front to form an open hearth giving access to the lead pot. The roof of the cabinet sloped upwards on all four sides ending in a circular chimney which took away the fumes and some of the heat generated by the red-hot pot.

Only non-stainless, carbon steel trade knife blades were processed in the hardening shop, these were butchers', chefs', and shoe makers' knives. Stainless steel blades were sent out for processing to a Little Mester, Wilf Croft, who specialised in stainless steel hardening and tempering.

The other equipment consisted of a tank full of whale oil, and a further tank containing chemical salts which were heated to a temperature suitable for tempering the hardened blades. Without tempering they would have been brittle.

The hardening process was fairly simple. Using a pair of tongs to hold them, blades were placed into the molten lead, the pot could hold approximately thirty-six butchers' knife blades, standing upright, at any one time. Only the blade part and approximately one centimetre of the tang were heated for hardening, this was because, in a later process, the tangs had to be drilled which would not have been possible if they were hardened. After reaching the correct temperature, two blades were removed from the pot, placed in a clamp and then immersed in whale oil. This quenched the blades much more slowly than water, so preventing cracking. Several sets of clamps were in use at any one time and, as quickly as two blades were removed from the pot and transferred to the whale oil, they were replaced by two others and so the process continued.

Once fully quenched the first clamp was removed from the whale oil and the blades taken out and placed in the tempering tank, here they slowly heated up to the temperature of the salt it contained. Once removed and allowed to cool slowly the blades were still hard yet flexible.

The day of the non-stainless trade knife seems to have passed, but, in my opinion, no modern stainless steel knives, even those with molybdenum added, can compare with the old, double-shear, carbon steel when it comes to cutting quality. My wife still uses a carving knife and a paring knife with double-shear steel blades for preparing and carving food.

Trade knife blades being quenched in whale oil for hardening.

During the day many of us would pop into Scouse's hardening shop for a chat and a smoke, Scouse had the gift of the gab, especially where ladies were concerned. He became particularly fond of Rosie and she of him, so much so that after work some extra curricular activities began to take place. It came as a great shock to Rosie, and a much greater one to Scouse, when she found herself pregnant. After that the buffer lasses, who always had some outrageous remarks to make on everyday events, called the hardening shop the softening shop. But all's well that ends well, Scouse and Rosie were soon married and lived happily ever after. (To save embarrassment after all these years, I have changed their names.)

To the side of the hardening shop was a short, narrow passage on the right of which a door led to the grinding shop. This low-ceilinged room contained two, Walters and Dobson, grinding machines, an open-fronted Sheffield type, sixty-ton blanking press, a powered guillotine, pedestal grinder and two modern W. & D. double-header glazing machines—which were a great improvement on the belt-driven ones I had previously worked on. The only heating in the shop came from an open fire situated at one end and, as the grinding shop was partly below street level, the only windows were fairly high up along the left hand side, facing Mary Street at pavement level. Because of this they were protected by permanently fixed wire mesh guards which not only prevented them from being cleaned but also from opening.

What with the fumes from the glazing machines, water splashing around from the grinders, permanently working in artificial light and the appalling noise that constantly assaulted our ears, the grinding shop was not a pleasant place in which to work.

With full employment at that time people could pick and choose what job they wanted, they seldom chose noisy, dirty jobs in manufacturing industry and who could blame them? This kind of working environment was probably one of the contributory factors to the start of the decline in British industry.

Enterprise Works was a tenement factory, housing several small firms. It was the property of, or they could have been the main lease-holders of, a company called The Rockingham Plate & Cutlery Company Limited, which was owned by two delightful characters, Cyril and Percy Potter. The name Potter was well known in Sheffield cutlery manufacturing circles. In the 1920s they had owned a factory in Boston Street where several of the workshops were let to Little Mesters. Earlier, I mentioned the story of a fire that had ruined several rented workshops, the re-equipping of these and the ensuing sale of this new equipment to a local dealer to provide Saint Monday boozing money. Potter's factory was where this had taken place and the equipment had rightfully belonged to them.

Modern machinery took the hard work out of knife grinding and quickly led to a vast reduction in the number of hand grinders and Little Mesters. Most modern grinding machines would only grind knives with a blade length of up to nine inches but, uniquely, I believe, one of our Walters & Dobson grinding machines had been specially adapted to grind large 12-inch butchers' and chefs' knives. Trade knives are measured by the length of the blade, a twelve inch knife being almost eighteen inches long when the handle is taken into account.

At that time, when many independent Sheffield steel companies were producing a vast range of special steels, we were able to buy a few tons of ingots, either stainless or carbon steel, and send them for rolling to Johnny Wood's rolling mill at Loxley. This small company would gladly take on jobbing work. There, our ingots would be rolled to the thicknesses we required, the whole cycle taking only a few weeks. This facility gave us a very competitive edge and back in our workshop the steel could be guillotined to whatever width required for the knives being made, which ranged from two-inch paring to twelve-inch butchers' knives, these were then punched out on the blanking press.

Another reason, in my opinion, for the loss of competitiveness in the Sheffield cutlery industry was that, after the first nationalisation of the steel industry, many independent steel firms disappeared and rationalisation became the 'in' word. One effect of this was that quite soon the nationalised steel companies would no longer supply small users like ourselves, preferring to deal only with large stockists who, incidentally, often did not stock the type or size of steel we required.

One such stockist was Walker's of Blackburn, where Mr Walker, the owner and benefactor of Blackburn Rovers football team, made his millions. This is not meant to be a criticism of the new system, or of Mr Walker, it probably made good commercial sense for British Steel to produce hundreds of tons of one particular steel and supply it to various stockists around the country. The stockist could then sell it on in small quantities, at inflated prices, to anyone wanting that type of steel, at that particular thickness. For anyone wanting a specification not carried by the stockists, it was just too bad.

Although this is jumping a long way ahead, I feel it appropriate here to mention that in 1973, when on a fact-finding tour, I visited Tsubame, the cutlery manufacturing city of Japan. One of the interesting things that I discovered was that slap bang in the centre of the manufacturing area was a rolling mill. Here, my Japanese competitors could purchase ferritic, martensitic and austenitic stainless steels, in relatively small quantities, rolled to the thickness and pared to the width they required, with just two or three weeks for delivery, exactly as we in Sheffield could do prior to nationalisation.

This was a wonderful facility that had not been available to Sheffield manufacturers for many years and, more importantly, the price they were paying was less than half the price I had to pay for similar steel in England and in Ireland where we then owned a second factory. It galled me even more when I tried to place an order for some of this inexpensive steel for use in our own factories only to learn that, under EEC regulations, the Japanese were not allowed to sell stainless steel sheet to EEC countries, except at EEC prices. However, there was no such regulation to prevent them selling the finished cutlery, made from stainless steel costing half the price their European counterparts were forced to pay.

Considering, for example, that in our Irish factory, almost 50% of the cost of producing an inexpensive stainless steel teaspoon was in the cost of the raw material, in this case stainless steel sheet, there is little wonder that we lost our competitiveness. To be specific, the cheapest ferritic stainless steel sheet that we could buy was made in France. To obtain the best possible price we were required to place firm call off orders for over 100 tonnes annually, at a special price of £490 per tonne. My Japanese competitors were paying £242 per tonne, for quite small amounts, without having to commit themselves to annual contracts.

One tonne of two-millimetre-gauge stainless steel sheet would produce just over 2,000 dozen teaspoons, therefore, my raw material cost was approximately 24 pence per dozen, whereas for my Far Eastern competitors it was only 12 pence per dozen. On top of this is the processing cost and even if our processing costs were no more than those of our Far Eastern counterparts we could not hope to compete. Sheffield manufacturers often found themselves in a situation where they could not buy the raw material for the price at which the finished product was being imported. For EEC regulations to deny us access to raw materials at the same price as our Far Eastern competitors, and at the same time allow the finished product to be imported from foreign countries free of duty was, in my opinion, the politics of madness.

To make matters worse, if that were possible, British Steel appeared to have badly mis-calculated the demand for certain types of stainless steel. As mass-produced stainless steel spoons and forks became more popular, replacing the inexpensive chromium plated ones that were produced in large quantities in Sheffield by companies such as Billam's and Sippel's, it became clear that the material being used was ferritic stainless steel. This type of steel derives its stainless properties mainly by the addition of chromium during the melting process. It is inferior to austenitic stainless which contains both chromium and the much more expensive nickel.

British Steel concentrated on the latter and I recall that when we last tried to buy Sheffield-made ferritic stainless steel sheet, preferring this to that of any other EEC country, we were quoted two years delivery, which really meant they were not interested. Much against our will we were forced to buy French or Belgian material. My estimate is that of all the stainless steel spoons and forks sold throughout the world during the last thirty years, probably 80% are made from ferritic stainless steel. Furthermore, whether they are manufactured in Japan, China, South Korea, Taiwan, Hong Kong or any other Far-Eastern country, which is where most inexpensive cutlery is now made, the steel will most likely have been produced in Japan. Was this miscalculation one reason for the loss of jobs in the Sheffield steel industry?

In 1948, in the grinding shop, I had a roving commission which enabled me to learn how to set up and operate the grinding machines and the blanking press, both jobs being new to me. This knowledge was to stand me in good stead in later years. It was unusual for a small manufacturer to produce his own blades, as these were usually made by specialist companies whose end product was a hardened and tempered blade. Most manufacturers bought their blades from these companies who, over a long number of years, had built up huge stocks of expensive blanking tools covering literally hundreds of different shapes and sizes. For trade knives there were only a few such companies, Samual Staniforths being the largest.

One small company that I vividly recall consisted of only one employee, namely the owner, Mr Davy, whose premises were in Napier Street. Inside his extensive, extremely clean and tidy workshops were several presses, furnaces, drilling machines, a guillotine, an eccentric rolling mill and other equipment, all ancient machines belt driven from line shafting. Davy, as he was known, also bought, in addition to the standard 6' x 3' sheets, off-cuts from shovel manufacturers. The specification of the steel was quite good, with a high carbon content which was ideal for the smaller sizes of butchers' and boning-knife blades. By paying a little more than the scrap price, and performing every operation himself, Davy was able to offer trade blades at very competitive prices. Even though we then produced our own blades there were certain ones we still bought from Davy.

Tiger's S'trip

Tiger worked on the first floor in the buffing shop. The buffer lasses, who shared the same workshop, were always singing, some of the songs having their original lyrics substituted for their own bawdy ones. Tiger, whose taste in music consisted mainly of songs from the old musicals, 'Desert Song' being one of his particular favourites, often joined in. To say he had an unusual voice would be an understatement. Whilst not quite falsetto it was rather high-pitched but what made it unique was the warble, or flutter, that came out every time he sang. His efforts were always greeted by raucous encouragement from the buffer lasses.

The works' outing, which was enjoyed several times a year, was a regular highlight of those carefree days when everyone really let their hair down. I well recall one such trip to Skegness when, having set off early in the morning with the coach loaded up with every kind of drink imaginable, everyone was nicely relaxed when we arrived at our destination. With a short break for food and a wander around the pleasure beach and amusement park it was back to a local hostelry for some singing and dancing. On the way home it was customary to call at a pub or a night club to complete the festivities, the Sportsdrome, in Bolsover, was one of our favourite stopping-off places.

Many of the Sportsdrome's regular clientele were miners and their wives, who always made our jolly crowd welcome. At one end of the room was a small stage where the three-piece band provided the musical entertainment. This was mostly for dancing but was often interspersed with 'turns', some professional, but anyone could get up and sing and often did.

On this particular occasion, Tiger, who by now could be realistically described as well-oiled, was prevailed upon to give us a song. After some discussion with the band, and a few false starts to sort out his right key, Tiger launched into one of his favourite arias from the Desert Song, 'O-o-o-o-o-o-one al-o-o-o-o-o-ne, to be-e-e-e-e my o-o-o-o-own'. On reaching the last line, with his Adam's apple bobbing up and down like a demented MP

A Housley Works' trip, 1955. Tiger is in the centre on the back row.

seeking the attention of the Speaker, the applause was terrific with repeated cries of 'More! More! Encore! And, it must be said, one or two 'Ger im offs', from the odd few who did not appreciate the finer points of a singer of Tiger's calibre!

By this time Tiger, who after many years of serious practice, could hold his drink like a good 'un, was really beginning to feel the effects of the booze he had been consuming all day and could not, for the life of him, remember the words of any other song. Not wanting to let his audience down, they were still demanding an encore, Tiger suddenly thought of Gypsy Rose Lee, the famous stripper who was all the rage at the time and, after da-di da-ing her theme tune to the band, he started to emulate her routine. He started off by removing his jacket, thus revealing his mucky army braces and, as it was a special occasion, he was wearing a collar and tie, those articles came off next. By this time the band were really into the stripper music and, with the audience shouting encouragement as he danced around, off came his braces quickly followed by his boots and socks.

Now the place was almost in hysterics, especially as his trousers had fallen down revealing the John L. Sullivan underwear, that Tiger apparently wore all year round, bearing the tell-tale, black fingermarks round the flies, caused by not wiping the black buffing grease from his fingers when visiting the loo whilst at work! Just as he started to undo the top buttons of his John L's, the owner, who had been watching the proceedings from the side of the stage and joining in the laughter and encouragement, suddenly realised the implications the finale might have on his licence and he speedily brought the performance to a close—much to the disappointment of some of the ladies in the audience. As Tiger returned to his seat to don his clothes he received a standing ovation.

There was a sequel to this event, when, on his return to work the following Monday morning, Tiger told us that when he arrived home after the day trip, he found his father, who was well turned eighty, laid on the sofa with a female companion, both of them having done a Gypsy Rose Lee! What really upset him though was the fact that the lady in question was none other than Audrey, who was supposed to be his own girl friend. Such is life!

People and Pastimes

My father had always been fond of a drink and the companionship of his pals in the pubs he frequented. In all the years that I worked with him he never missed going out for a drink every lunch time. The trouble was that quite often these lunch hours lasted for the rest of the day. Not only did he celebrate Saint Monday, but often Saints Tuesday and Wednesday as well.

Some of my father's closest friends at that time were the Wilsons, whose family business was L. Wilson and Sons Limited, Cutlery Manufacturers. Dad had done knife grinding for them for many years and the owner, Lawrence Wilson, had two sons, Gordon and Tony. When he diversified into tool manufacturing he named the tool company after his eldest son. Gordon Tools Limited became a household name for spanners and other small tools shortly after the war.

Lawrence had a brother, Leslie, who managed the Machete knife department. He was a delightful, well educated man, always smiling and, with his refined accent, he seemed a little out of place in the pubs he frequented with my father and other grinders. He loved to play my father at cribbage but seldom won.

Gordon and Tony were amongst Dad's regular lunchtime drinking companions, as were several priests from the nearby St Vincent's church and school. Two of the pubs they frequented, both in Broad Lane, were the Barrel Inn and the Newcastle Arms. The former was known as 'Fagan's' and the latter 'Gaffey's', after their landlords. Gaffey's has long since disappeared but, in recognition of his long and popular years as mine host, and to commemorate his memory, the name of the Barrel Inn has been officially changed to Fagan's and his portrait incorporated into the pub sign.

In the days when pubs were compelled to close at 3 pm some very serious drinking took place at Gaffeys which often continued 'after bird'—outside legal drinking hours—and into the evening session. Playing crib and solo for relatively small stakes and backing horses must, together with the general patter, often have helped the participants to lose track of time. Apart from after-hours drinking in the afternoon, many's the time my father stopped off at Gaffeys for a 'livener' on his way to work at 8 am, either to join or be joined by Gordon or Tony who were probably also feeling under the weather.

My younger brother, Barry, joined the firm in January, 1945, on leaving school at the age of fourteen. Of all the cutlery workers I have ever known Barry was amongst the most skilful and hardest working I ever met. When I returned to work, Barry was still only sixteen and worked in the cutlers' shop, drilling, riveting and glazing trade knife handles. Two middle-aged married cutlers, Ivy and Ada, the latter better known as Merrylegs on account of her bandy knees, worked alongside Barry and tended to mother him.

We were producing large quantities of butchers' and similar trade knives during that period, all of which had wooden handles. Rosewood, beech, redwood and, quite rarely, ebony, being some of the timbers used. The handles were called scales, and the blades were known as scale tang blades which, being drilled without the use of jigs to position the holes, meant that every pair of scales had to be individually drilled to coincide with the position of the holes in one particular tang, this was known as matching. The scales were then riveted to the tang by means of wire, sometimes steel and sometimes brass. This was bought by the coil, cut into lengths of approximately ten inches, then straightened and had points ground on one end.

Each riveter had a tiny anvil inserted into his bench which had a V-shaped slot at the front. The wire was first tapped through the top scale, then the tang and finally the bottom scale. The V-slot allowing it to pass right through. Once the end of the wire was flush with the top scale a serrated knife was passed underneath, the wire partly cut and then snapped off. Depending on the number of holes in the tang, which could vary from three to five, this operation was repeated and then the wire was burred over on the anvil, using a small hammer, which permanently fixed the scales to the tang.

Afterwards the wooden scales were shaped by hand on a coarse, dry, grindstone then glazed on a broad leather-covered buff, previously coated with abrasive carborundum grit and subsequently fine-glazed on a similar buff. This applied mainly to the cheaper timbers such as beech or ash, the more expensive timbers, rosewood being the most popular, received still finer glazing and a final wax polish on a soft, calico mop.

It may seem unbelievable now but, having purchased the sheet steel and the handles and undertaken some fifteen separate manufacturing operations, in 1947 we sold carbon steel shoemakers' knives for 6s 6d per dozen, less than 3p each in today's currency.

Although we were now fully fledged cutlery manufacturers we had virtually no direct customers of our own. My father had always been a Little Mester undertaking grinding, buffing, cutlering (hafting) and polishing for other manufacturers. Now, even though we were making the complete article, he still sold to other manufacturers who simply etched them with their own names and sold them on—a bit like the supermarkets own brand system of today.

Lawrence Wilson & Co. Limited who, by now, had given up cutlery manufacturing, and their subsidiary company Gordon Tools Limited, had a thriving home and export market. Gordon Wilson often undertook extensive sales trips abroad returning with pockets bulging with orders. The years immediately after the war were great years for the British manufacturing industry. Many of the orders they received were for cutlery and trade knives which were placed with manufacturers such as ourselves. One such, very large, order was for sisal knives to be used on the ill-fated 'groundnuts scheme' in West Africa. They were a peculiar shape, the double-curved redwood handles were held in place by three brass compression rivets, and they were particularly difficult to cuttle or haft. (The word 'cuttle' as used in the Sheffield cutlery industry, referred to the fitting and finishing of the handle. The person doing this work was a cutler, and the workshop where this was undertaken was the cutlers' shop.) The sisal-knife order took several months to complete and, despite dust extractor fans, the inside of the cutlers' shop became covered in fine redwood dust in no time, as did the hair and clothing of everyone in that workshop.

Fresh water fishing had long been the most popular outdoor activity of Sheffield grinders, a welcome Sunday break from breathing in the dust-laden atmosphere of a grinding wheel. This goes back to the days of the charabanc, my father often spoke of going fishing in a covered wagon, not the wild west type, but an early lorry with solid rubber tyres, fitted with temporary slatted wooden seats and covered with a canvas canopy in case of rain.

My own fishing activities began as a young lad when, for our one week annual holiday, we were always taken to Boston in Lincolnshire. In 1935, at the age of nine, I remember climbing with my brother Charlie, the dark, winding, 365 stone steps, one for each day of the year, of the Boston Stump—the enormous gothic tower of St Botolph's, the local parish church. On the flat Lincolnshire landscape it can be seen from miles around, and was to become a landmark for aircraft returning from bombing raids during World War II. On a clear day, Skegness, twenty-two miles away, can be seen from the top.

Before the days of pollution by nitrates, pesticides and herbicides the River Witham was a Mecca for Sheffield anglers, it simply teemed with fish of many species, big black bream being the favourite quarry. Archie Webster and his wife Gertie, a buffer lass, used to accompany us on holiday and it was Archie who taught me how to fish. Having no children of his own Archie had great patience with youngsters and was prepared to forgo some of his own fishing pleasure to teach us the rudiments of the sport he loved. I could not have wished for a better or more skilful teacher.

Annual works or pub fishing matches, strictly men only at the time, were popular events looked forward to for months in advance. For some of the participants it was their one and only fishing experience of the year, for them the words 'fishing match' meant a glorious booze up. I well remember one such event which took place at Keadby—the river Trent, the navigable Keadby canal and other waterways are quite adjacent to this small Lincolnshire village. Our party, from the Victoria pub in Addy Street, were fishing a drain with steep banks; another match from an Attercliffe pub were fishing the opposite bank. With all the banter that was taking place between men out for a good time and people tramping up and down both bank sides, who could blame the fish for not biting.

As soon as the local pub opened, a general exodus of casual fishermen, the majority of those present, took place. About three hours later, slightly the worse for wear, they began to drift back. A young man fishing on the opposite bank to me slipped down the steep bank ending up, to howls of laughter, with his feet in the water. For most people a drink brings happiness and bonhomie. To this foul mouth it had the opposite effect. He eventually recovered composure and settled down with fishing rod in hand only to find that the hook had snagged on the bottom. He reeled in the slack line and began tugging to try to release the hook. As his efforts failed, his swearing and tugging became stronger until both the line and his temper snapped.

He removed his reel, threw it into the middle of the drain shouting, 'Effin' fish can have that'. He then dismantled his fishing rod and smashed it across his knee. As he threw the pieces after the reel he shrieked, 'And thi can have that an' all'. The bait tin and ground bait followed and finally his fishing basket was thrown into the middle of the cut, there to remain partly submerged. Our hero then stormed away shouting, 'That's my effin' lot wi' effin' fishin''. By this time we were all falling about laughing, all thoughts of fishing having disappeared. The whole episode had been better than watching a slapstick comedy.

On another Sunday, together with five friends from the Bagshaw Arms, we were fishing the river Wreake in Leicestershire, near to the village of Thrussington. This was one of our favourite venues where, on adjourning for a spot of light entertainment, we had become friendly with some of the locals in the village pub. The day was sunny but bitterly cold and, having left Sheffield in the early hours, as soon as the pub opened for the two-hour Sunday lunch-time session, we were in.

Four of us soon started playing darts, the two losers standing down to be replaced by the two sitting out. It was not long before two locals challenged the winners and, 'to make it more interesting' they suggested we play for a pint. What they didn't know was that most of us played for the Bagshaw darts team in a local league. Needless to say we kept on winning. Not wanting to cause offence by quitting the game whilst in front, our table was soon covered in pints. By the time the lunch-time session was over we had consumed more than our fair share, none more so than Ken Baldwin, our best player.

On returning to the river bank we were soon seated on our fishing baskets engrossed in trying to catch some of the large roach and chub that the river Wreake contained. Sugars, despite spectacles with lenses as thick as milk bottle bottoms, was quite a good angler. He was fishing close to a tree whose branches overhung the river. By casting his line short of the nearest branch and letting the float drift downstream he had done very well during the morning session. Sugars' casting judgement was not so good during the afternoon and the tree began to take on the appearance of a decorated Christmas tree as many of his colourful floats became entangled in its branches.

Suddenly there was a terrific splash, we all looked up thinking someone had caught a big fish. It turned out to be Ken who, having nodded off to sleep on his fishing basket, had fallen into the river head first. Coughing and spluttering he scrambled to the bank and we pulled him out. It was still very cold and sunny. Without more ado Ken stripped of his wet clothes (the full Monty) and, whilst he was not as well endowed as some, his dangly bits flopped about wildly when he started running up and down the bank side trying to get warm.

We rubbed him down with a dirty cloth covered in sticky ground bait and someone generously offered him a full-length black oilskin coat to cover his embarrassment. As quickly as possible we packed our tackle and returned to the pub, knocking on the back door for admission. When we told the landlord what had happened he was just as amused as ourselves and kindly loaned Ken some warm dry clothes. Not to be outdone, his wife started cooking us a meal which, when ready almost two hours later, proved to be one of the most memorable I have ever enjoyed.

Another member of our party was Billy Lees, a middle-aged widower who, the following Saturday, was due to marry Aggie, a widow of similar age. To keep ourselves in the ladies' good books we had arranged to meet them in the Bagshaw Arms at 8 o'clock that evening. A fatal error. By the time we had eaten the delicious meal it was already 7.30, the pub had re-opened and, not wanting to cause offence, we stayed for a drink—just the one. Needless to say, one led to another and it was almost closing time before we embarked on the return journey to Sheffield—this was before the breathalyser was invented. The vehicle was a Ford Utilicon, a kind of seven-passenger mini-bus in which the seats folded down to create a useful delivery van, which is what I used it for during weekdays. I was driving and before many miles had passed, all I could hear was the snoring of my passengers.

It was after midnight before we arrived back in Sheffield, needless to say all the ladies were back at their respective homes. We were all in deep trouble, none more so than Billy Lees who never went fishing again.

I am not sure who owned Enterprise Works. It may have been that Sheffield City Council had bought it under a compulsory purchase order in anticipation of building the inner city ring road that now covers the site. The main tenant, to whom we paid rent for the workshops we occupied, was a company called The Rockingham Plate & Cutlery Company owned by Cyril and Percy Potter, two unforgettable characters who could have come straight out of a Dickens novel.

They often placed business with us but seemed to have problems when it came to payment. On once occasion I was entering the factory just as Cyril, in his smart pinstriped suit, was coming out.

'Tell your father to come and see me, immediately. There are several orders considerably overdue that I must speak to him about.'

'Yes, Mr Potter, I will.'

When I gave my father the message he said 'If you want a laugh, come with me; and it'll do you no harm to learn a bit about business'.

We arrived, both clad in our normal boilersuits, Cyril and Percy, both smartly dressed, were seated at their polished, mahogany desks in a well-furnished office. This was a far remove from the small alcove, containing two three-legged cutlers' stools and a rough wooden bench, that passed as our office.

'Hello, Cyril, what can we do for you today?' was my father's opening remark.

'Come in, Housley, and young Housley, have a seat.' Neither Cyril nor Percy ever used Christian names or the word Mr when speaking to tradesmen. 'Now then, Housley, these delays in fulfilling our orders are just not good enough.'

'But we're still awaiting payment for several lots of knives we supplied you with months ago' was fathers exaggeratedly hurt reply.

'I've told you to contra what we owe you against the rent you pay' Cyril responded.

'I've done that with some even older accounts and we're about twelve months in advance with rental payments already.'

'It's still not good enough, Housley' and, turning to me with a wink, he went on, 'don't you think your father is an awkward man to do business with young Housely? We shouldn't be kept waiting so long. I'll tell you what, I'll get Percy here to write you a cheque and you can collect it when you next make a delivery to us.'

'Oh, reight, Cyril, I'll send our Herbert across with some stuff on Friday but instead of a cheque make it cash. I'll let you know how much when I get back. By the way, he'll have strict instructions not to leave anything unless we receive the cash we've agreed on.'

After a bit more of this routine the interview ended with honours even. These old, yet friendly, adversaries whose dealings went back many years knew how far each could go without causing offence or breaking the unwritten rules. Father knew that the Potters were struggling to make ends meet and would pay whenever they could.

Cyril was a severe asthmatic, with a porcelain-like complexion and was often struggling for breath. They came from a bygone era and had not come to terms with their straitened circumstances.

Sad to say, their company, was to go into receivership a few years later, and the Manager, Frank Tomlinson, who was put in by the liquidator, was to play an important part in my future career. However, Cyril and Percy were resourceful old characters and the next thing I knew they owned another cutlery company called Bunting, Langdon and Company Limited, based in the same premises and using the same offices and showrooms as their former company. What's that about coming up smelling of roses?

Wedding Bells

Before joining up I'd had a string of teenage crushes and a few girlfriends whilst in the Navy, but nothing serious had developed until I met Margaret Moore, at the Abbeydale Ballroom, whilst on leave. Our courtship was a stormy one, both of us being strongly independent and thoroughly enjoying our own different lifestyles. Margaret was part of a crowd of young people who enjoyed hiking, dancing, tennis and youth clubs. I had several drinking pals who often met in pubs or working men's clubs. We would also go to cinemas and the Empire Theatre. Our visits to dances were always preceded by a few drinks in the old Dove and Rainbow which was situated across Hartshead, not far from the present one. On the night I met Margaret, who was with two other friends, my pal, Bob Price, and I invited them to have a drink during the interval in the nearby Broadfield Hotel and the invitation was accepted. We were both on leave and wearing civvy clothes at the time. When I met her the next evening wearing my Navy unifrom she told me she would not have agreed to a date if she had known I was sailor.

I was serving on *HMS Rajah* when we met, we wrote to each other almost every other day and, when on leave, we had some great times. Margaret drank very little and did not smoke when we first met, and I must take the blame for encouraging her to take up these habits. My circle of friends, who enjoyed a few drinks and a singalong before going to the dance, were a happy-go-lucky lot and she soon became Maggie to the gang. We even persuaded her to dance on a table in the Dove and Rainbow one evening.

Margaret's parents lived at 30 Glover Road, Lowfields, two tram rides from where I lived in Upperthorpe. After walking her home we'd have a cup of tea and do a bit of courting, not the same as in today's liberated society, but enjoyable just the same—and many's the time I missed the last tram and had to walk home.

We met in 1946 and continued our courtship after my return to civilian life, eventually I plucked up the courage to ask her to marry me. New engagement rings were in short supply, and left a lot to be desired, so Margaret eventually chose a second-hand one from a small family jeweller whose shop was near to where she worked. It had been made in France before the war and, though it took all my savings to pay for it, the ring was quite beautiful. We became engaged in September 1947 whilst I was working at St Mary's Road but my independent streak, or was it the arrogance of youth, was to result in me leaving my father's employment shortly before we were married.

As previously indicated, my father spent almost as much time in the pub as he did at work. During his absences a few employees, who were supposed to be his close friends, took the opportunity to skive, often disrupting others from getting on with their own work. My younger brother, Barry, was fully aware of the situation but, at the age of sixteen, could do nothing to prevent it. I've often felt that he worked harder than ever to try to make up for the duplicity taking place behind Dad's back.

I soon realised what was happening but had no authority to prevent it, nor did I feel able to speak of my fellow workmates to the boss, even though he was my father. This led to ill feelings and cross words between this small minority and myself which ended in a scuffle with one of them. He struck the first blow but I was able to give better than I received. The fracas was quickly over and, there and then, I decided I would not put up with this

My wife to be, Margaret Moore, taken around 1946

intolerable situation and decided to leave forthwith. I never went back to work at Enterprise Works and, at the time, really believed that I would never work for my father again.

My best man to be was Bob Price who came to work for my father at St Mary's Road, shortly after I did. When I walked out he also left. I suspect it may have been out of loyalty to me but have never asked.

My future wife, who had worked in the offices of scrap merchants Marple and Gillot Limited since leaving school at the age of fourteen (her father worked there for 52 years), was surprised to learn that just a few weeks before our marriage, in July 1948, I was out of work. I was still living with my parents in the small back-to-back house, two up and one down, in Portland Street and my action led to a tension at home that could be cut with a knife with Mum trying to 'Keep t'cart on t'wheels between them two' as she often remarked.

Next day I went to R.F. Mosley's and asked them for a job. It was there that my father used to rent a grinding wheel and where, in 1939, I first started work in the cutlery trade. The manager of the knife department, I think his name was Mr Trickett, was known to me as a kindly man who knew knife manufacturing inside out. I was aware that they had recently purchased a Walters and Dobson grinding machine and two double-headed glazing machines, my dad's brother, Uncle Joe, who had taken over the grinding wheel when my father gave it up, had mentioned it in the pub a few weeks earlier. I told Mr Trickett that I was looking for a job and asked if there was a vacancy in the new machine grinding department.

'I'm sorry, old son, but the quality from the new-fangled machine is just not up to our standard. We were the first company in the whole world to manufacture stainless steel knives and have a reputation to consider. We only produce tip-top quality cutlery and silverware.'

'Just let me come and work on the new machines for a couple of weeks, without pay, and if the quality is still not good enough it will have cost you nothing' I responded. 'If, on the other hand, it's up to your standards then we can negotiate a piecework price, which is the way I prefer to work.'

'Well, those damn machines did cost us a pretty penny and they are laying idle. When do you want to start?'

'Will tomorrow be OK? I'm getting married in a few weeks' and with those words my new job commenced.

In retrospect, I believe that R.F. Mosley's traditional hand grinders, especially the foreman, a proud Sheffielder, genuinely believed that the introduction of grinding machines was a threat to the reputation of that company. Consequently, they did nothing to help the management to integrate the new machines, which were situated in a separate workshop, into the production schedules. Having started my working life in a grinding wheel I could understand this attitude. No machine at that time could equal the hand grinding of the best Sheffield workmen.

However, times were changing. There was a shortage of skilled labour and, with a few exceptions, my generation was probably the last to take up this type of work. In actual fact, only a very few of my age group have 'worked in't t'wheel'. Another reason why the new machines were lying idle was lack of knowledge. It was not particularly difficult to train someone to operate the machines but few people had the knowledge or experience to set them up. This was something I had recently learned at St Mary's Road.

The leather-covered, wooden, blade buffs used in the grinding wheel were painted with hot glue and then rolled in abrasive grit and allowed to dry overnight. A buff dressed in this way might last for an hour or two then it would be quickly replaced by a newly dressed one. This is why old photographs of grinding wheels show lots of buffs hanging in racks all around the workshop.

The glazing wheels used on a double-header machine presented a different problem. They were, roughly, 75cm in diameter by 5cm wide, (30" X 2"). They had an 8cm cushion of tightly compacted calico segments inserted, under pressure, into the steel wheel which was specially machined to accept them. The calico segments were, afterwards, turned true by the supplier who was based in Birmingham. These wheels were very expensive but, provided they were treated correctly, lasted for years.

The application of glue and abrasive grit to these glazing wheels was a skill that few people had mastered but, before joining up, I had been taught by an expert in the field. The wheel was first given a coat of thin, piping-hot glue which had to soak right into the calico and be left to dry for a few hours. The technique was then to mix the glue and abrasive grit together to the right consistency and to paint it onto the calico whilst hot. This had to be repeated three times at, roughly, hourly intervals. The buffs then had to be baked for several days in a warm drying-cupboard. When newly-coated glazers were first put on to the machine, gentle pressure and great patience was needed to ensure that the abrasive coating did not overheat, otherwise the glue would blister and the coating flake off and everything had been in vain. Nevertheless, patience did pay off and, when broken in correctly, they could last for up to two weeks. So, with the arrogance of youth and being aware of the foregoing, I was confident of my ability to make the double-heading machine produce ground and glazed blades to the required standard.

In 1948, rationing of almost every commodity was still in place. With the furniture ration coupons allocated to couples about to marry, we bought a utility bedroom suite, a drop-leaf table and four chairs. We also bought a second-hand sideboard and a utility Axminster carpet which also did sterling service in two subsequent houses. A lot of derogatory remarks were made about utility products, but the government imposed strict quality standards and price controls on all these items which were, in fact, excellent value for money. Most of the non-utility products, which were not subject to government controls, were a rip off.

In addition to food, clothes were still strictly rationed when we married, everyone being allocated a number of clothing coupons. Parents and grandparents were often persuaded to part with some of theirs to their children. Whilst I was in the Navy, on board ship, we were allowed to purchase tinned fruit, cooked meats and other foodstuffs from the NAAFI canteen. As far as pay would permit, I had been storing up these items—half of which were given to my mother—and, although it was jumping the gun, the rest saved for our wedding.

Margaret had bought a length of off-white cloqué material which a dressmaker friend fashioned into a magnificent wedding dress with a long train. Light blue satin dresses, also made by the family friend, were for the four bridesmaids and the maid of honour (Margaret's married sister, Dora, who was expecting her first child) and a white, satin suit for the young page boy. When I was demobbed I had opted for sports coat and flannels but these were hardly appropriate to get married in. Therefore, I had a navy blue pinstripe suit made by Joe Solity, an excellent tailor, working from a tiny workshop on Arundel Street. Bob, my best man, was similarly attired.

Two days before our marriage my wife was rushed into hospital to have a benign tumour removed from her arm. It had become inflamed and greatly enlarged, following a knock she received when the tram she was getting ready to leave suddenly swayed violently. We thought the wedding would have to be postponed but, following the operation and after being kept in overnight, she was allowed home.

Despite all the trauma, our wedding, on a brilliantly sunny day, was a most happy event with all my family disagreements forgotten. St Barnabas, Highfields, was Margaret's Anglican parish church, the venue of our wedding. Arthur Revill, the vicar, was a kindly man who toiled ceaselessly for his flock, indeed it may have been overwork that led to his premature death. The sincerity of Arthur Revill shone from his whole being and any young couple fortunate enough to have him conduct their wedding service, were indeed blessed.

One of my wife's friends was Norma Young, a local amateur operatic singer with a beautiful voice, she later turned professional. Her stage name was Sylvia Norman and she appeared on TV several times. Norma sang one of our favourite songs in church and sang others later at the reception which was held in the function room of the old S. & E. Co-op in Wolseley

Wedding day photographs, July 27th 1948

Jim and Nellie Moore, my wife's parents, Aunt Lilly, Grandma Housley, my parents and Uncle John.

Road, Heeley. If someone had told me then that some forty years later the building would become a mosque, I would have told them to pull the other leg.

Despite his drinking and gambling my father was an extremely generous man who loved his children. As a belated twenty-first birthday present he had bought me a car, a 1938 Morris 8 Tourer, which I promptly christened 'Pompey Lil'. After our wedding we stayed the night at my wife's parents' house and the following day set off in Pompey Lil for our one-week's honeymoon in Rhyl.

The job at R.F. Mosley's proved to be far less demanding and better paid than my former one at St Mary's Road. In fact, I was working 9am–4pm with no Saturday mornings—less hours than my wife who had opted for part time work! I had obtained permission from my boss to employ and train a young man to work for me, paying him out of the generous piecework prices I had been able to negotiate, once Mr Trickett approved the quality of my work. The only other

Margaret enjoying a drink outside the Hotel St Jean, Chalons-sur-Marne, 1949. The car was christened 'Pompey Lil'.

person in our department was Ernest Webster, an employee of Mosley's who was also the shop steward. Ernest operated the grinding machine whilst Bill, my young assistant, and I worked on the two double-header glazing machines.

Having spent my savings on an engagement ring, the only other money I had when we married was my £75 gratuity received after four years naval service. For the first year or so of our marriage, due to the acute shortage of houses, we lived with my wife's parents, paying a small rent for the use of the front parlour and back bedroom. Margaret's sister, Kathleen, had to sleep in the attic which was a bit of an imposition but it had its compensations as I took her to the football match every time Wednesday were playing at home.

We bought our first house, in Yardly Street near Weston Park, in 1950. It was a six bedroomed, terrace-type with slop kitchen, lounge and front parlour downstairs with two bedrooms and an attic above. It also had two coal cellars, coal being the only form of heating. It cost £400 and to help to pay for it we took out our first mortgage of £200. It was in a poor state of repair and we spent almost as much as it cost in renovations and decorating. The only running water was a cold water tap over the sink in the offshot kitchen. In there we installed a bath, boxed it in and fitted it with a hinged lid which we could close and use as a work surface. For hot water we had an Ascot geyser with a swinging arm that could deliver water to the sink or the bath. This was the first house that either Margaret or I had lived in with a bath—but we still had to use the outside toilet across the yard.

The Prodigal's Return

My father and I both suffered from stubborn pride, a trait that, unfortunately, runs in the family. It therefore came as a great surprise when, approximately one year after walking out of St Mary's Road, my father asked me to return to work for him.

Once again he was expanding and he had opened another department in yet another tenement factory, this time at 41 Arundel Street. The windows faced the rear of the Lyceum Theatre but, due to extensive redevelopment, this part of the city is now totally changed.

The year was 1949. My agreement to rejoin the firm, a decision that did not take long to make, was conditional. First, that my brother Barry and I should become equal partners with Dad, and second, that I became manager with overall responsibility for running the business. Father quickly agreed to these conditions and a partnership agreement was drawn up. We became H. Housley & Sons, Cutlery Manufacturers. In practical terms Barry and my father continued to manage the St Mary's Road operation, where the initial stages in cutlery manufacture took place, whilst I was given complete freedom to get on with things at Arundel Street. Thus began forty years of hard labour and huge responsibilities, yet it was a wonderful opportunity for a young man. At the age of 24 my first faltering steps at running a business had commenced. I made plenty of mistakes during the ensuing years, all of which were paid for either in cash lost or disappointment. There is no better teacher than experience.

Once again I found myself in decrepit old premises which were awaiting demolition, after being compulsory purchased by the Council some years earlier, to make way for the inner city ring road. There was the inevitable archway whose walls housed a conundrum of electric meters, wires, fuseboards and switchgear, some live others dead—an electrician's nightmare. I say this knowingly because many years later I met Doug Maw, a foreman electrician with YEB whose area at that time included this factory. He told me what an almost impossible task it was when called out to a fault, which happened regularly, to sort out which equipment belonged to the various tenants spread around the factory. The whole installation should have been condemned but, as each tenant could be evicted at any time subject to only three months notice, no-one could be expected to pay the high cost of rewiring.

Our workshops were well scattered around the factory. The ground floor ones were on the frontage, with second and third floor ones leading off the yard at the back. This led to an enormous amount of fetching and carrying of heavy boxes full of cutlery up and down many flights of narrow stone steps.

The front door of 41 Arundel Street, next to the archway, led into a dark hallway illuminated by a single light bulb. Once inside, to the left, a flight of stone steps led up to our office and the warehouse which extended over the top of the archway and had windows facing the street, the office overlooked the yard. To the rear of the hallway were three doors. The one on the left was the entrance to a whitewashed unisex toilet underneath the stairs, the centre door led into the yard. The right-hand door opened into a small storeroom used for packing-cases and cartons ready for despatch and for storing packaging materials. Just inside the room, a large steel-covered trapdoor opened to reveal more stone steps going down to the cellars where coal and coke were stored to fuel the fireplaces in the various workshops, our only form of heating.

Although a notice instructed anyone using the trapdoor to bolt the door into the hallway, I can recall at least one occasion when this was not done. Someone going into the cellar had left the hall door open and a driver delivering a large bail of woodwool, used for packaging, walked through the open door and fell straight down the open trapdoor. Fortunately, the woodwool broke his fall but he still suffered cuts and bruises.

A final door, this time to the front of the hallway, was the entrance door to our spoon and fork filing shop at street level, immediately underneath part of the warehouse. Here we employed three filers, Jack Wright was the foreman who tried manfully, with little success, to keep Alice Campbell and her more sedate workmate, Emily Boulby, under control. Jack and Alice were totally different characters who reacted to each other like cat and dog. It was an education to observe some of their antics. Jack had served in the 'forgotten army' in Burma. I believe this was a traumatic experience for all those gallant men who fought there, having to contend not only with the Japanese but impenetrable jungle, snakes, insects and a host of tropical diseases. I think the experience affected Jack's health. He was gaunt and pale, but he never complained or had time off, he was a quiet person who just got on with the job in hand. He was exceptionally skilful and, apart from army service, had spent all his working life as a filer.

Alice Campbell was one of my all-time favourite characters. Although she was a filer, for me she typified Sheffield buffer lasses, hard working and drinking, often swearing, but this was really part of their everyday language and no disrespect was intended. When I first met Alice she was approaching middle age, still an attractive woman with her hair, which had a centre parting, combed back off her forehead giving her the appearance of a demure schoolmarm—but no one could have been less like a schoolteacher. She had a ready laugh and her many facial expressions indicated, without the need for words, what she was thinking—which was usually disrespectful.

Walt Webster, our long-serving foreman cutler, by the fire exit of our Arundel Street cutlers shop. The top of the Graves Art Gallery can be seen in the background.

Before describing spoon and fork filing I should first explain how the blanks were produced and, whilst on the subject, perhaps also describe the forging of knife blades. Until the 1950s most spoon and fork blanks were made from nickel silver, an alloy of copper, nickel and zinc. In some parts of the world, Argentina for example, this alloy is known as alpacca and, as there is no silver in nickel silver, I have never understood why it is so called. The amount of nickel, which is very expensive, used in the alloy varied enormously from as low as 5% used for some silver- and chrome-plated spoons and forks, right up to 30%. The lower the nickel content the more yellow it was in colour, whilst the higher the nickel content the more silver its appearance. After being silver plated it is known as EPNS, (electro-plated nickel silver) whereas with old Sheffield Plate the silver was fused onto a copper base, with EPNS the silver is deposited electrically.

Years ago the blanks were crude compared to those of today. The flat, nickel-silver sheet was stamped out to the outline shape of the spoon or fork design required. This was done with hardened steel blanking tools of which there were a large number of different shapes and sizes. In the case of spoons, the bowl had to be thinner than the rest of the item, otherwise it would have been uncomfortable to use. To achieve this, the initial spoon blank was oval-

Nickel silver spoons being lowered into a plating vat for electro plating (EPNS).

shaped at the bowl end. This was then rolled out and, afterwards, the bowl was clipped to its correct shape under a power press—a bit like cutting out pastry for jam tarts. Fork prongs were pierced out similarly in a separate operation.

In some instances a heavier section was required on the handle near to the spoon bowl or fork prongs. This was achieved by 'stowing', the cut blank was placed on its edge between specially shaped dies and placed under a drop stamp. The resulting blow, when the heavy tup was released from a height of six to eight feet, would increase the thickness of that part of the handle. A drop stamp looked a bit like the French guillotine and was equally lethal, as many stamp operators with missing fingers could testify.

After the blanks had been cut and stowed the next process was to stamp the design into the handles, this was also done under drop stamps. Kings,

1. *The initial shape of the spoon, cut from sheet metal.*
2. *The end has been cross rolled to form the bowl.*
3. *After 'clipping' the final bowl shape, the handle is coined with the design under a drop stamp.*

Spoon bowls being 'clipped' under a power press.

Queens, and Bead being typical examples of designs made. The spoon or fork was placed between two hardened-steel dies into which the design had been cut in reverse then smoothed and polished.

Die sinking, as the cutting of dies was called, was a highly-skilled craft. The most intricate of patterns would be cut into steel dies by hand using simple tools. A hammer, small chisels, specially shaped files and a pointed wooden stick and emery powder, used to polish the dies, were the main tools used, many of which were made by the die sinker. Coins have their design impressed in a similar way and this operation is often referred to as coining. When, some years ago, I visited the Cairo museum and saw the mask of Tutenkahmen and hundreds of other artefacts, it struck me that many of the tools used by the ancient Egyptians to create such magnificent works of art were not dissimilar to the simple tools used by Sheffield die sinkers during my lifetime.

Spoon bowls were similarly formed, again between two dies under a drop stamp and when I mentioned earlier that the blanks were crude it was no exaggeration. As the spoons or forks were being stamped, excess metal was forced out to form a thick burr, or 'flash' as it was known, it was the filer's job to remove this. In earlier times this was all done with steel files, indeed for sterling silver we still used hand files to remove the flash and all the filings were saved, but for normal blanks fine grindstones were used. Even so, just after the

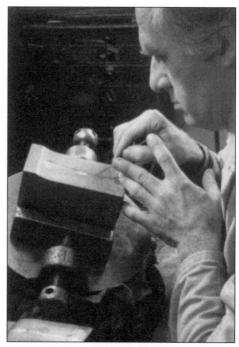

A die sinker working on a fork handle die.

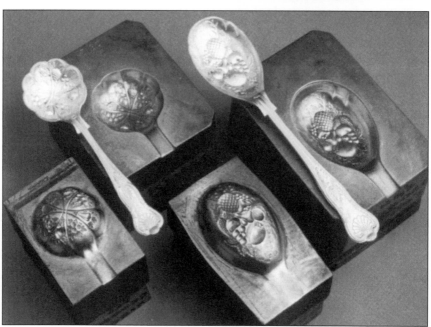

Examples of top and bottom spoon bowling dies. Using simple tools the intricate designs have been hand-carved by a die sinker into solid blocks of steel.

The bottom half of a modern, full length fork-forming die. Previously, separate dies were used to form the handles and prongs.

1. The initial blank is cut from sheet metal.
2. The prongs are pierced.
3. The handle is coined with the design.
4. The final contours of the fork are formed, the 'gate' or bar, joining the tips of the prongs is removed and the prongs are ground.

last war, scrap dealers would buy the dust from the dust extractor to recover the non-ferrous metal filings.

The blanks were still flat after stamping, so the filer had to set the handles and fork prongs, (set is the word used to describe the curves on spoon and fork handles). On forks the pip at the end of the handle had to be set upwards (pip up) and on spoons downwards (pip down). This is to prevent the end digging into the hand during use, spoons being used with the bowl upwards and forks with the prongs downwards. Sets could vary enormously from that of a soup ladle to a tiny mustard spoon. With a little help from a fly press holding the appropriately shaped bending dies which were used to set the curve, setting was done using primitive tools. These were shaped by the filer from pieces of buffalo horn to prevent the pattern being damaged whilst the handles were being bent and hammered to the correct set in the vice. The crude hammer-head was also made from buffalo horn by the filer.

The insides of the prongs, which also contained flash, were ground and tapered to a point using very narrow grindstones known as 'pronging wheels'. Great care had to be taken to prevent these very thin and fragile grindstones, which were revolving at high speed, from being broken. When a pronging wheel did break it sounded like an explosion and resulted in fragments of stone flying in all directions, despite the steel safety-guards intended to prevent this.

'Filing' the insides of fork prongs using a narrow grindstone.

Flat dinner fork prongs being 'rounded' under a heavy drop stamp between a pair of curved steel dies. Setting the contours of handles and prongs used to be done, by hand, by the filer.

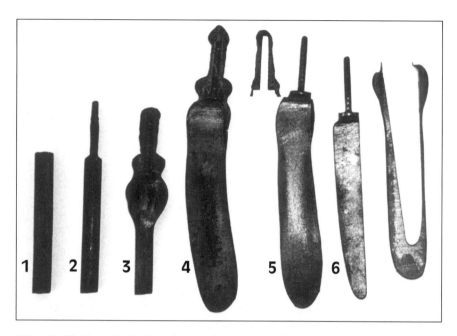

The Sheffield method of producing forged knife blades.
(Still current when I retired in 1985, despite modern methods introduced elsewhere 30 years earlier.)

1. Short lengths (slugs) of stainless steel bar are cut to size while the steel is cold.
2. After heating to 1000°C the tang is partly formed under a spring hammer then allowed to cool.
3. Heated again to 1000°C then the bolster and tang are formed under a drop stamp then allowed to cool.
4. Heated again to 1000°C, the slug is elongated between eccentric rollers. As stainless steel cools it becomes very hard.
5. After annealing for many hours in special ovens the excess metal around the tang is removed.
6. The blade shape is then trimmed—note the excess metal produced from each trimming operation. The blade must now be re-heated and placed in a die to align the tang, bolster and blade.

This process is an ancient and inefficient method of hot forging. Using tongs, the slugs are placed, one at a time, side by side, in an open-hearth furnace. On reaching the required temperature, the operator performs one single task, then throws the slug down, forming a random pile on the floor. After cooling, probably the next day, they are collected up from the pile and taken to another part of the workshop. The heating process is repeated, one operation is performed, and once more they are piled on the shop floor...and so it goes on. To reach stage 6 shown in the illustration, the parts will have been heated to 1000°C on four separate occasions, been collected from the floor five or six times and will have been moved about from one area to another—a terrible waste of energy and resources.

The modern method was reported more than 30 years ago in the magazine of the Cutlery Research Council. The chairman of the Council, who managed a cutlery forge supplying blades to the majority of Sheffield cutlery manufacturers, was however, of the opinion that the methods he continued to use were the best. The rest of the world disagreed. One or two of the forward looking Sheffield manufacturers who had their own hot-forging plants did change to the modern method.

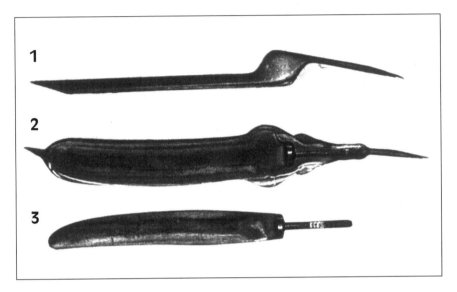

A modern method of knife blade forging.
1. *Using thick stainless steel plate, the first operation, performed whilst the steel is still cold produces the 'mood' shown—a powerful blanking press is required. The components are collected mechanically and stacked neatly in trays ready to be placed in magazines for the next operation.*
2. *After slowly passing through a, magazine-fed, walking beam furnace (a long narrow furnace which gradually moves the components from one end to the other) the components reach the required temperature for forging. Using a very powerful 600-ton friction screw press, and three impression forging dies, the mood receives three separate blows which form tang, bolster and blade in seconds.*
3. *After annealing, using full-length trimming tools, excess metal is removed from the blade, tang and bolster in one operation.*

The Cutlery Research and Allied Trades Association (Bulletin 59, 1969) described the entire process with great clarity and detail using photographs taken at a factory in Solingen Germany. Amongst the advantages described were, better quality blanks, less gauge variation and excellent alignment of tang, bolster and blade. The misalignment of blades, due to outdated forging techniques, is something that has plagued the Sheffield cutlery industry for many years. It continues to this day.

A modern three-impression die which produces the tang, bolster and blade after just one heating.

In 1972 I was privileged to be invited to visit a modern factory in Solingen, Germany, where I was shown their own development of modern knife blade forging. Two knife blades are produced from one forging, this is a technique other Sheffield cutlery manufacturers may yet be unaware of—the saving in energy alone is enormous.

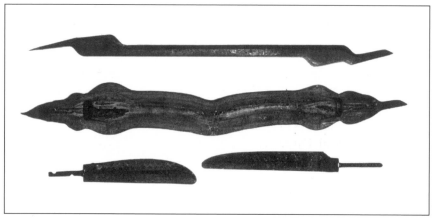

A German method of producing two knife blades from one forging.

A speciality of Jack's was in the making of tanged fish-eaters. The tang is that part of the blank to which a separate handle of another material, often mother-of-pearl, is attached. In addition to fish eaters and servers, jam and sugar spoons and small butter knives were some of the items included in this range.

Separate bolsters made from nickel silver were crudely cast in strip form at a brass foundry. After being separated on a guillotine, they were hammered onto the end of the tang using a round piece of steel with a hole, big enough to pass over the tang, drilled down the centre. To fasten them securely to the blank the 'tommied on' bolsters were pressed between a pair of dies under a heavy-duty fly press. Once secured, the bolster had to be ground, freehand, on all surfaces to clean up the surface and produce the shape of the finished bolster from the crude casting and also to ensure a good fit between the bolster and the handle.

The backs of the bolsters were milled on the most primitive belt-driven machine imaginable. Years later when this type of bolster was superseded by precision cast ones, I realised that this machine was a piece of Sheffield's industrial heritage, and the only one known still in existance, so I gave it to the Kelham Island Industrial Museum.

Next time you see a set of white- or pearl-handled fish eaters in an antique shop, think of all the work involved in just producing the bolster.

Mother-of-pearl, found mostly in the tropics, is a substance which lines the shells of many molluscs, oysters being the best known, it is similar in nature to the pearl itself. Its beautiful iridescence and lustre are due to an optical phenomenon, the interference of light.

Pearl Divers in the Persian Gulf and the Gulf of Manaar off the coast of Ceylon (now Sri Lanka) collect the shells during a short fishing season lasting from four to six weeks. A stone weighing about forty pounds (18 kilos) is attached to the cord by which the diver is let down. They work in pairs, one man diving whilst the other watches the signal cord. On the signal the sinkstone is drawn up, then the basket containing the shells and, finally, the diver himself. On average the divers remain underwater for fifty to eighty seconds during which time, in addition to his hands, the diver makes skilful use of his toes. To arm himself against the attacks of sharks he carries spikes of ironwood and no genuine Indian diver descends without the incantations of shark charmers. Despite this, as a rule, the diver is a short-lived man. (Incidentally, Pearl Diver was the name of a horse that won the Derby shortly after the war—we won a few bob on him.)

Around 1960, May and Baker, the drug company, introduced through a subsidiary company dealing in plastics, an imitation mother-of-pearl material which they called Nacrolaque. This was made, I believe, from a mixture of cellulose, acetate and other ingredients. It was supplied in sheet form and could be purchased in various thicknesses by handle manufacturers. When cut into blocks, shaped into handles and polished it became an excellent substitute for the real thing and at a fraction of the price. Using this new material I designed our first exclusive range of cutlery which we called 'Pearlcraft'. In the ensuing years many more designs were to follow. Pearlcraft proved extremely popular and during the next two decades sold well in both the home and export markets.

I have often heard the term 'bone-handled' used to describe cutlery with white handles but bone was never used as a handle material during my working life. Some of the natural materials that were used included ivory, buffalo horn and stag horn. The latter enjoyed great popularity in the export market, particularly to the USA. I had limited experience of using ivory, mainly in replacing damaged handles belonging to old and treasured sets, and also when removing non-stainless blades from ivory-handled knives to replace them with stainless ones—a decision I would not have made, but the customer was always right. Ivory, which has a very fine grain, comes mainly from the male elephants' tusks and is really an enlarged tooth. In years gone by it was used extensively in the cutlery trade but, thankfully, there is now a total world-wide ban on its use.

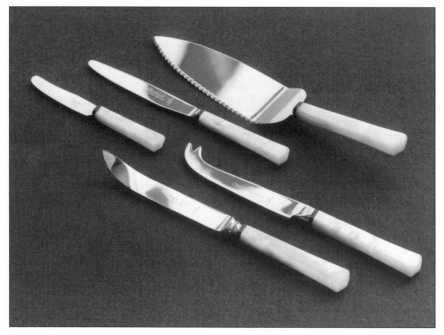

'Pearlcraft' the first exclusive range of cutlery I designed.

Xylonite (celluloid) is, I believe, a trade name belonging to BX Plastics Limited. This material was also supplied to the handle manufacturers in sheet form of varying thicknesses. The handle maker would, firstly, using a circular saw, running in water, cut the large sheets into strips and then into oblong blocks. The width of strip and thickness of the material depending on the type of handle to be made. The blocks were then made into handles of a multitude of shapes and sizes to suit the type of knife. Xylonite could be purchased in three qualities: common white, which had a slightly pink cast; best white; and white grained. The latter was probably intended to simulate the appearance of ivory. Celluliod is very highly flammable and is a compressed, solid solution of nitrated cellulose in camphor.

Xylonite is no longer used for knife handles. New, safer materials, some even dishwasher-safe, have been introduced. Cellulose acetate, acrylic, nylon, polypropylene and polystyrene are some that spring to mind. Instead of being fabricated from large sheets these materials, in powder form, are injection moulded so enabling the most intricate shapes and detail to be incorporated. Typical examples of current usage of these materials are in kitchen, butchers' and chefs' knife production.

In recent years the concept of co-ordinated tableware designs has resulted in plastic handles being decorated to match the design on china, stoneware, place mats, table linen, dishes and other table-top items.

When I took up my duties at 41 Arundel Street, our warehouse was staffed by three women whose job it was to inspect, wipe clean, and paper-wrap in dozens, or gift-box in half-dozens, all the finished cutlery. They were also responsible for checking in and counting the partly finished products from the various workshops, including those at St Mary's Road. These were, eventually, issued to our other workshops for final finishing as and when required.

Edna Weston specialised in table knives and also operated the Taylor Hobson electric etching machine, situated in a cavernous adjoining room. This room had originally consisted of two storeys but one floor had been removed. It was extremely draughty and cold in winter, the only heat coming from a large tortoise-stove in the centre of the room. The electric etching machine, a standard piece of equipment in practically all Sheffield cutlery factories, worked on the pantograph system. It had, more or less, replaced the much slower and costly acid-etching process. Some traditional companies, R.F. Mosley for example, still acid-etched all their knives and there is no doubt that a much better etching mark resulted. For our best quality products we used the services of a Little Mester specialising in this process whose name, I think, was Mr Fry.

Using a circular saw, revolving in water to prevent sparks (xylonite was highly flammable) a sheet of xylonite is cut into oblong blocks ready for shaping.

Using specially shaped steel cutters the oblong blocks of xylonite are shaped into knife handles.

The Taylor Hobson etching machine electrically etched fifteen knives simultaneously. A master plate, usually made from brass or xylonite sheeting, was fastened to the table of the pantograph. The operator, by following the grooves cut into the master plate, and at the same time depressing a switch, etched the knives. One or two firms specialised in making etching plates. All one had to do when ordering a plate was to provide the detail required. This could be a trade mark, a shipping line's crest or just the name of the company for whom the knives were being made. The detail was cut into the master plate either by hand or with the help of a special engraving machine.

The knives being etched were held in place by a jig and the etched mark was produced by tiny copper javelins tipped with fine platinum wire. When the knives were in position the javelins were lowered so that they came into contact with the blade. With the right hand the operator placed a stylus into the grooves cut into the etching plate and at the same time depressed a switch with the left. This caused the javelins to vibrate rapidly causing a spark which burned into the steel. The vibrating javelins sparked continuously whilst the switch was depressed and the operator had to use great concentration to ensure that the stylus remained in the grooves cut into the master plate. Should the operator allow the stylus to slip out of the grooves, then fifteen knives would be spoilt and need re-polishing, a process which involved several glazing and buffing operations. The cursing and swearing from the polishers, when asked to remove faulty etching marks, was sufficient to ensure that the operator took great care to try to avoid these confrontations.

I recall that Edna, our etcher, had served in the forces during the war. She came from a close-knit family and was the sister of Merrylegs who worked at our St Mary's Road factory. A slim attractive and very caring young woman, Edna was not yet married nor, at the time, did she have a regular boyfriend. She was rather highly-strung and suffered from a peptic ulcer which required all kinds of special powders and diet to control. As an employee she was most conscientious and formed an important part of our team for several years until she eventually left to marry.

Rita Kitten, not her real name, was the warehouse manageress and also the mistress of one of my father's friends. He was a well-known local manufacturer, long since dead, who will also remain anonymous. Georgie, the lover boy, was a regular afternoon visitor to our warehouse after the pubs closed. He used to stand in front of the fire holding Rita's hand and gazing into her eyes for lengthy periods of time. This was not a situation which fascinated me at a time when I was just starting my managerial career and had an awful lot to learn about tact and diplomacy—I still do for that matter.

Rita already resented my presence. Georgie's company placed quite a lot of business with my father and because of this she tended to give the

A Taylor-Hobson electric etching machine, which etches fifteen knives simultaneously.

impression that she was outside my authority. However, I had learned my lesson at St Mary's Road and, after a few weeks, I politely told her that what she did in her own time had nothing whatsoever to do with me but whilst at work she was expected to do just that, work. No doubt she reported the conversation to Georgie, who stopped his visits, but it was never mentioned to me by anyone. Shortly afterwards she left our employment of her own accord. We didn't lose any business though—where else could Georgie get a better deal?

Kath Buttery, an extremely attractive and vivacious married woman with two young boys, also worked in the warehouse. She was to remain a key employee and family friend for many years to come. I had been a keen angler since boyhood and when Kath's youngest son, Trevor, grew up we also became good friends and often went fishing together on Sundays. However, once the golf bug bit, I gave up fishing and have seen very little of him in recent years but feel sure our friendship remains.

In the same room as the etching machine were two floor-mounted, motorised, buffing spindles used for knife buffing and whetting. I spent quite a lot of my time working on one of these spindles. Whilst working I was usually mentally keeping track of all jobs in production and planning everyone's next job, including my own. Harry Hewitt worked alongside me,

Young trainees pose for a photograph, taken in about 1950, outside 41 Arundel Street.

he was a chirpy character who always had a fag-end hanging out of the corner of his mouth—he had a terrible cough. Sometimes he entertained the warehouse staff with a bit of impromptu clog dancing on an upturned metal tray, a hobby at which he excelled. It became his party piece when we called at a pub on our works' outings.

In a partitioned area of this large, high-ceilinged room Tommy, our spelter bolster expert, worked all alone. He had an artificial leg, after a childhood accident resulted in his leg being amputated well above the knee. He welcomed a job that required him to be seated all day. He kept budgerigars which he loved to talk about whenever anyone went into his room.

Mention of Tommy reminds me of 'Budgie t' cat killer'. Budgie was a young steelworker who went out with us, occasionally, before I joined up. He had acquired his totally unwarranted, bloodthirsty reputation from his great love of a family pet which he often talked about, a little, green, talking budgerigar. It was often allowed the freedom of their small back-to-back terraced house to fly around and it allowed our friend, Budgie, to feed it whilst resting on his finger. The neighbour had a moggie whose sole aim in life appeared to be to catch and kill next doors' budgerigar. One day, by sneaking into Budgie's house when the door was open and by lying low, it succeeded.

When Budgie came home from work he was devastated and blew his top. Grabbing the first thing that came to hand, which happened to be a poker, he dashed outside waving the weapon in the air and shouting obscene remarks that no self-respecting cat could possibly have understood. The chase was quite one-sided and, needless to say, the cat escaped. By then however, the die was cast and from that day to all the neighbours he became 'Budgie t' cat killer'.

Budgie had another dubious claim to fame, this time as a result of his great patriotism. Shortly after the Japanese attack on Pearl Harbour the propaganda ministry was urging the nation to still greater efforts, especially the steel workers. Budgie worked in a steel-rolling mill where the windows fronted onto a stretch of the River Don, opposite a main road along which buses and trams regularly passed to and fro. He had been reading a Ministry of Information poster, on the works notice board, containing the words 'Remember Pearl Harbour'. These words really struck a patriotic cord with Budgie and he decided that they should have a wider audience. During his lunch break he obtained a pot of white paint, scrambled down onto the river bank and proceeded to paint the words from the poster in three foot high letters under the firm's windows. All went well until he reached the word harbour, then some doubt set in regarding the correct spelling. As time was running out, and him being a resourceful chap, he quickly completed the sentence which finally read 'Remember Pearl Dock'!

There are different types of blades used for table cutlery. The more expensive ones are hot forged from stainless steel bar, the bolster being an integral part of the forging. The cheaper blades are made from sheet steel and are known as 'whittle tangs' shades of Chaucer's *The Canterbury Tales*, and the 'Sheffield thwitel' which the Miller of Trumpington 'baar in his hose'. These blades needed to have a bolster fitted separately. Until the advent of precision die-cast bolsters, around 1960, molten spelter (zinc) was poured into a pair of small dies into which a whittle-tang blade had been inserted. The spelter quickly set around the blade tang forming a bolster, the size and shape of which depended on the die being used.

The spelter bolster then had to be ground and polished by the cutler prior to the handle being fitted. I recall that in the late 1940s and early 1950s we sold fully finished whittle-tang table knives for approximately 12/- per dozen (5p each in today's currency). When one considers the materials needed, stainless steel, spelter, a handle, plus almost twenty manufacturing operations, there is no wonder that the cutlery workers were so poorly paid and that there were so few successful post-war Sheffield cutlery manufacturers.

Christine Ryan was our book-keeper and secretary responsible, amongst other things, for wages, invoicing, purchases, cash book and correspondence. In a small business this kind of versatility was the norm—and probably still is.

Chris was a beautiful young woman with a gorgeous complexion, ready smile and a gentle personality but had the misfortune of being badly crippled from birth. About a year after I joined the workforce at Arundel Street she left to marry a serving airman. By a coincidence I knew her family who, before the war, lived in Upperthorpe, her brother being in the same class as me at school. Her father was a well-known local eccentric who gave his profession as that of an inventor although hardly any of his inventions went into production. The only invention I know of, which received a lot of publicity in the Star at the time, was a flat-topped kettle on which other items could be placed and heated whilst the kettle was being boiled, thus saving fuel.

Across the yard, on the third floor, our cutlers' shop was run by Walt Webster, an experienced and hard working cutler, who was to remain with our company until retirement some thirty years or so later. He was ably assisted by Beatty Foster and her sister-in-law Mary Willey—it is amazing how many members of the same family used to work together in the cutlery industry. A fourth member of the team, who joined straight from school a year or two after I took up my duties, was Roy Davies. He was a diminutive youngster, less than five feet tall and weighing about six stones wet through. We had to provide a box for him to stand on to reach the glazing wheel. Roy remained with us for many years.

The cutlers, who, unlike the grinders, did their work standing, had to grind, glaze and polish the bolsters and backs of the blades, after which the handles, which first have to be drilled and countersunk, are fitted. Once fitted, the handles were buffed on a stiff calico mop, using wet, powdered pumice, then they were finally polished on a soft, calico mop. The penultimate manufacturing operation was to polish the blades. To protect the handles from being scratched whilst the blades were being polished, they were individually wrapped in newspaper by the warehouse staff who also inspected them at the same time.

The cutlers also had to undertake some work on the solid one-piece knives, as used in school canteens, by the forces and many municipal catering establishments. They also had to glaze the backs of the old fashioned, whittle tanged, bread and salad knife blades to which were fitted turned wooden handles complete with a ferrule-type bolster. At that time we produced thousands of whittle tanged, serrated, bread knives which were fitted with coloured wooden handles before being individually boxed in printed cartons. We ordered the cartons in lots of 20,000 which gives you an idea of how many we made.

The most expensive knives that the cutlers had to prepare were fitted with hollow, nickel silver, handles which were stamped (coined) to match the

Mary Beckingham who retired in 1989 at the age of 73. She spent 58 years in the trade, mostly with H. Housley & Sons Limited.

Using only hand and eye, staghorn handles are drilled freehand.

Solid, one-piece, stainless steel knives

A typical cutlers' workshop. The upright steel stanchions, called puppets, held small wooden blocks which acted as crude bearings for the pointed steel axles of the belt-driven buffs.

designs on the spoons and forks. These handles were made in two halves and then soldered together. They were produced by just a few specialist firms whose only manufacturing operation was the production of hollow handles for the cutlery and surgical instrument trade. These manufacturers also hard-soldered the hollow handles to their customers' own blades. After buffing and polishing, the hollow handles were silver plated. Sterling silver knife handles were also made this way. The heat generated by the soldering process could create an area, just up from the bolster, that was susceptible to corrosion. It was known as 'band corrosion' and, for many years, caused the industry lots of problems. Nowadays, instead of hard solder, a cold cement is used to fit hollow handles and that particular problem is eliminated.

All the equipment in the cutlers' shop was belt-driven from line shafting running under the bench. The glazing buffs and grindstones were mounted on steel spindles, pointed at both ends and fitted with a small wooden pulley that the leather belt ran in. Small oblong wooden blocks, roughly 6" · 3" · 1", into which a small hole was burned with a red hot poker, were the 'bearings', for want of a better word, that the pointed ends of the spindle ran in. The wooden block was placed in a slightly larger oblong slot in a cast iron stanchion called, a 'puppet' which in turn was held in place by a ring bolt and tightened by a small tommy bar—usually an old sharpening steel. This was a most primitive, yet quick and effective method of transferring motive power from line shafting to the many different buffs and glazers used throughout the day. The same method which had been in use for decades, if not centuries. It certainly dates back to the times when waterwheels were the source of power, as can be seen at Abbeydale Industrial Hamlet.

Although no jigs or mechanical aids were used, each bolster was virtually identical after undergoing several grinding, glazing and polishing operations, a tribute to the craftsmanship of the old Sheffield cutler who, just by sight, could detect and rectify minute variations in size or shape.

The second floor was occupied by our spoon and fork buffing, and knife polishing shops. Two of our employees, Kate Fox and Elsie McGowan, both in their mid-fifties, were typical of buffer lasses of that era. They both still celebrated Saint Monday, a practice that I, and most of the industry, had discontinued after the war. Kate, a short plumpish woman, was the mother of Kath Buttery who was her eldest daughter. She had several grown-up children and had worked hard all her life to bring them up. Her youngest son, Harry, also worked for us for a few years in the cutlers' shop. He left to become an ashphalter. The 'black stuff' could pay much better wages than the cutlery trade. Daughter Pat, and daughter-in-law, Jean, also came to work for us. They were quite a dynasty and a lovely, close-knit family.

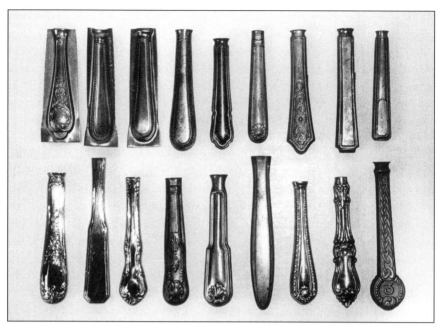

A selection of hollow handles. They are stamped in two halves, top left, then trimmed and brazed together.

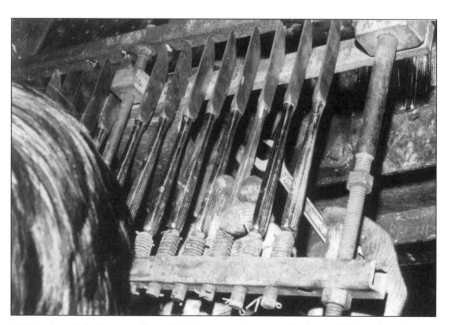

Hollow handle knives are aligned in jigs to await curing after being filled with cutlers' cement and having the blades inserted.

With her family grown up, her husband working and those children still living at home each contributing to the family income, I don't think there was still a need for Kate to come out to work, but buffing was a way of life much preferred to the kitchen sink. Kate only worked part-time and no matter how late she got to work she always managed to get away well before the pubs closed at three o'clock. She denied vehemently, to anyone unkind enough to harbour such a thought, that she ever went near a pub on the way home or even thought of doing so!

'What me? Call an' 'ave one on't way 'ome. Never! Chance 'ud be a fine thing. I've got shoppin' t' do, an' when I get 'ome a meal to cook an' t' washin' an' t' ironin'. I dun't know how tha' cud think such a thing.'

Full of contrition and knowing full well that she and Elsie always had a drink on the way home, I would apologise for even contemplating such a thing. This little cameo went on for years, especially when she was particularly late in and we had urgent work for her. Kate never once admitted, probably not even to herself, that she had a daytime drink, not even on Saint Monday. She really believed that she had convinced everyone, husband and children included, of her innocence. We all laughed about it as we kept up the pretence.

Kate was of Irish decent and loved to sing the Irish songs as she worked, her favourite being 'How can you buy Killarney?' Alice Campbell was one of her drinking pals and it is with feelings of great affection that I remember them both. They lived and enjoyed life to the full.

Les, a mirror polisher, who worked on the same floor, provided a different story. Drink had completely taken over his life. He only came to work to finance his alcoholism. He was an excellent mirror polisher earning good money but had let himself go. He came to work unshaven, his grey whiskers and red-rimmed eyes making him look much older than his fifty or so years. He must have suffered agonies from his daily hangovers. Like many heavy drinkers he ate very little and was quite thin and undernourished. Many people tried to help Les, myself included, for, despite his drinking, he was a quiet-spoken, likeable man. Nevertheless he seemed to be beyond rehabilitation and, after several years of bad timekeeping and absenteeism, drink finally took over completely and he just stopped coming to work.

Trade was quite good for several years after the war. The greatest problems for us being lack of supplies and skilled workers. The spoon and fork blank manufacturers introduced an unofficial form of rationing which favoured the old established companies—to the detriment of new ones like ourselves.

Hot-forged table blades were also in short supply, but, there were several blade forgers and it paid to deal with all of them, picking up whatever blades we could from all sources. So far as whittle-tang table blades, butchers' blades

The hand polishing of cutlery is still undertaken. This photograph was taken at Warris & Co., Mary Street, in 1998.

and other trade-knife blades were concerned, fortunately, we made our own at the St Mary's Road premises. We could, in fact, sell ground blades or finished knives to other cutlery manufacturers.

Generally speaking, the production of spoon and fork blanks required the facility of specialised, expensive, tools and dies and heavy machinery. An example of the latter was a cross-rolling mill used to thin down and spread spoon bowls prior to the final shape being cut out.

The number of items in a full suite of English cutlery was enormous. The fourteen basic items were: coffee, tea, porridge, soup, dessert and table (serving) spoons; dessert, pastry, table (dinner) and fish forks; table (dinner), dessert, fish, and tea knives—but these were only the basics. In many designs there were also salt, mustard, mocha, gravy, vegetable-serving, ice cream, fruit-eating, fruit-serving, children's, grapefruit, lemonade, sundae, jam and berry spoons. Salad servers plain and claw and fruit servers; sauce, cream, gravy, punch and soup ladles; fish servers, cake servers of many shapes and sizes. Sugar tongs; salad, grapefruit, cheese, bread, child's, fish and butter knives; fruit, oyster, snail and hors d'oeuvres forks; cheese scoops; lobster picks; carving knife, fork and steel; game carving knife and fork; steak knife—the list is endless. At some stage in my life I have made every one of the items listed, and more besides when trade knives are taken into account.

The minimum tools and dies required to produce just one spoon in one particular design are:

1. *blanking tool*–to press out the basic shape
2. *clipping tool*–to press out the correct bowl shape after cross rolling
3. *handle forming die*–to stamp the design into the handle
4. *bowl forming die*–to change the flat metal into a spoon bowl

Although some tools and dies could be used for more than one design, for example a dessert spoon bowl could be the same size and shape on different designs, not many tools were interchangeable and, therefore, the spoon and fork blank manufacturers had hundreds of tools and dies in their storerooms, weighing hundreds of tons in total. The cost of producing them, which took place over a long number of years, must have been enormous.

Most blank manufacturers employed their own, in house, die sinkers and toolmakers. They also made use of outside independent firms to supplement their own production, but supply never seemed to keep up with demand. Dies in particular were susceptible to wear and breakage, and were constantly being repaired or replaced. Shortly after the war there were well over two hundred cutlery manufacturers in Sheffield, most of them

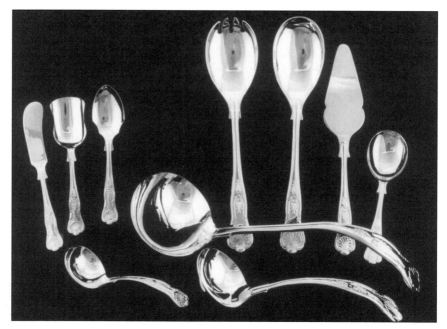

A selection of popular accessories, stocked by manufacturers in many different patterns.

purchasing spoon and fork blanks from approximately five blank manufacturers but not all of them offered the same designs. Indeed, some designs were exclusive to a particular blank manufacturer whilst others, known as 'parish patterns' were supplied by them all.

This could lead to problems for the cutlery manufacturer in that there was no standardisation. For example King's pattern teaspoons, from Turners (Eyre Street) Limited, differed quite a lot from the same design as supplied by Sheffield Metal Company Limited—we had to be extremely careful to ensure that teaspoons from different sources did not find themselves in the same set of cutlery. This was quite difficult when several batches were in the course of production in the factory and, afterwards, during plating. Quite often an irate customer would return a whole canteen of cutlery to a retail shop complaining that some pieces did not match.

Due to the prolonged shortage of blanks, most cutlery firms placed orders with all the blank manufacturers and accepted delivery of whatever was available. Because of the many different designs, and large numbers of items in each design, the blank manufacturers were forced into producing comparatively small batches, rather than a large output of one design—this must have made them quite inefficient. The volumes were there to be made but, if a blank maker had four hundred different items in his range and

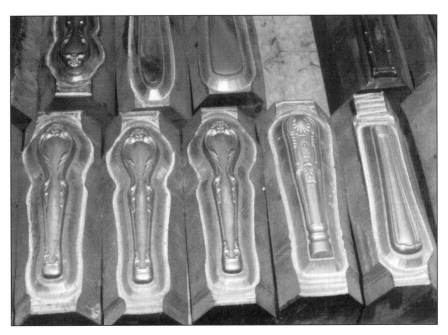

A small selection of dies for hollow handle knives.

produced, say, only ten items per week, it would take forty weeks before each item was made. Even a small company like ours would order a thousand pieces of the most popular items in several different designs. This could add up to sixty or seventy thousand pieces in total.

Traditionally, most Sheffield cutlers' price lists invariably offered a wide range of designs and items available in that design; blanks for which, before the war, could be purchased off the shelf from the blank manufacturers. However, with orders pouring in from home and abroad from customers who wished to replenish, or replace in the same designs (as used by hotels, shipping lines, restaurants and retail stores) the blank manufacturers were swamped—for some items they were quoting more than a year for delivery! Repeatedly, even such long delivery promises were broken. Chaos prevailed and Sheffield's reputation for reliability suffered. Manufacturers often found themselves with thousands of poundsworth of unfinished cutlery sets on their hands that could not be despatched because, for example, there were no dessert spoon blanks available. Inevitably, this led to financial problems that could not be resolved and the post-war decline in their numbers began.

Overseas buyers began to look elsewhere for supplies, countries like Australia, New Zealand and the United States turned to Japan and other Far-Eastern countries for alternative sources. Japan quickly began to copy

'Kings' pattern, a traditional Sheffield design copied by cutlery manufacturers

Sheffield's traditional designs but, instead of nickel silver, they used stainless steel. At first their quality was poor, but gradually it improved. They also offered modern patterns in sets consisting of a few basic items, these were often referred to as Scandinavian designs. Sweden and Denmark were thought to have led the rest of the world in the use of stainless steel as a material for the manufacture of high-class modern cutlery.

Some of the Scandinavian patterns were extremely well-designed and finished to a high standard. They were also very expensive whereas much of the cheap cutlery coming from Japan was badly designed and poorly finished. This tended to make the general public associate stainless steel with cheapness and held back the general acceptance of good quality stainless steel tableware which still persists to this day. Personally, I would much rather have high-quality, Sheffield-made cutlery of traditional designs in 18/10 stainless steel, rather than in EPNS or even solid silver, both of which need constant cleaning. You do, however, need to know what to look for.

What I have briefly tried to describe did not happen to the cutlery industry overnight but developed over several years. I believe that the inability of Sheffield manufacturers to maintain delivery promises, coupled with the spoon and fork blank manufacturers great reluctance to use stainless steel, marked the beginning of Sheffield's decline as a major world supplier of cutlery. Another important factor was, I believe, the proliferation of very small family businesses without the necessary capital to develop new designs and market them properly. They were often run by elderly people, set in their ways, who scoffed at the notion of modern materials such as stainless steel.

Around this time, in the mid 1950s, I wrote a letter to the Board of Trade to express my views on the state of the cutlery industry in Sheffield.

A personal assessment of the Sheffield Cutlery Industry as it is today.

This letter applies only to the table and trade knife section of the Sheffield cutlery industry, which is my area of expertise. Apart from a handful of larger units, to which the assessment does not apply, our industry consists of well over one hundred small, mostly family, businesses. They employ, on average, from ten to fifteen people.

All these small firms are not, in the true sense of the word, manufacturers. Without exception they purchase spoons and forks from three or four specialist blank manufacturers whose end product is an unfinished pressed blank. Similarly, rough forged blades are bought from two or three specialist blade forgers. The same remarks apply to specialist hollow handle makers, fabricated plastic handle makers, moulded plastic handle manufacturers, canteen cabinet makers and specialist silver plating companies.

Virtually no modernisation or mechanisation, let alone automation, has taken place in most of these small companies who continue to use the same methods of manufacture that have been used for hundreds of years. All their products rely on the hand skills and craftsmanship of individuals.

A high proportion of employees who are working on production are women. Their average age is over fifty, many are much older. This situation is probably the greatest problem that the companies, to whom this assessment refers, will shortly have to face. Generally speaking, since 1939, the beginning of the last war, women have not entered the cutlery trade as buffers or polishers. When the present employees retire, or leave the industry, there will be no one to replace them.

Where some small cutlery companies have achieved high volume production, the cutlery has invariably been of the cheap variety and quality has been sacrificed for quantity. Shoddy spoons and forks, stamped from non-stainless mild steel sheet are mechanically polished, then bright chromium plated. Cheap, so-called 'whittle-tang' knives, made from thin, bright rolled, stainless steel sheet, to which a superficial bevelled edge is ground, are fitted with cheap injection moulded plastic handles.

Unfortunately, these products bear the legend 'Made in Sheffield' and, in addition to the home market, are exported, especially to Commonwealth countries. In the writer's opinion, these products can only damage the priceless reputation of Sheffield cutlery gained through hundreds of years of fine craftsmanship.

Many small companies also make extensive use of outworkers, Sheffield's so called 'Little Mesters' who either work alone or have only one or two employees. Little Mesters tend to have their own speciality, such as blade grinder, cutler (hafter), buffer, mirror polisher, serrater, swager and so on.

It should be noted that every company has to support some kind of office staff to deal with the ever increasing amount of forms and returns that have to be dealt with. Selling organisations are conspicuous by their absence. The cost of supporting just one sales person, providing a car and paying hotel and travelling expenses is usually beyond the means of the smaller companies that this letter is concerned with. Selling trips abroad are almost unheard of. The cost of producing worthwhile illustrated brochures, especially coloured ones, is usually prohibitive.

The foregoing is, of course, only the writer's assessment of the Sheffield cutlery industry as it is today. If true, and I believe that it is, then it shows just how badly fragmented the industry really is. Unless the owners get together to achieve some form of rationalisation and integration, then, to say the least, the future looks bleak.

How to achieve rationalisation? There is no simple answer but, some form of amalgamation acceptable to several companies will have to be found if they are to survive. If such an approach was made from someone within the industry, it would probably be viewed with suspicion by the owners of the companies approached. If on the other hand the initiative came from a government body, such as the Industrial Reorganisation Corporation, then some concrete results may be achieved.

Many of the proprietors of these small companies are getting old and would probably welcome an opportunity of selling their business. Others will eventually die and their business will continue to be run, in the same old way, by their next of kin.

What is required is one large company, instead of dozens of small ones, housed in one, purpose built factory where every operation in the manufacture of knives, forks and spoons takes place. A central administration unit would replace the dozens of small offices that currently exist. The group would be able to commission the best tableware designers, produce first class literature and advise nationally, possibly internationally. A sales director and area sales managers should also be part of the organisation and top officials should make regular selling trips abroad.

The amount of capital needed for one company to take over a score or so of the most forward looking, small cutlery manufacturers, build a new factory and fill it with the most modern plant and equipment is beyond the reach of anyone that I am aware of. On the other hand, the time is probably right for such an amalgamation to take place and, if wheels could be set in motion by an independent body, I believe genuine interest would result.

As a result of this initiative, a meeting of interested companies was subsequently arranged through the auspices of the Sheffield Cutlery Manufacturers Association. About six small companies attended the meeting but nothing ever came of it. Needless to say, my worst fears were to become reality and practically all of the hundred or so manufacturers I wrote of were to disappear.

I began to realise that the situation I have described would cause us nothing but problems in the future and decided to rationalise drastically our own product range. Wherever possible I wanted to be independent and not have to rely entirely on blank suppliers for everything I needed to produce.

Fish eaters, with white or pearl handles, were then popular gift items. They could be supplied in EPNS or chromium plated and did not require the use of a cross-rolling mill. With our existing equipment we could actually produce our own tanged fish eater blanks.

My father had some contacts with scrap dealers who frequented some of the pubs he used and we were able to buy scrap copper and nickel from them. We already had a quota for zinc which was needed for our spelter bolster production. This meant we had everything necessary to produce our own nickel silver. A local firm, whose name I have forgotten, turned these materials into nickel silver ingots and then rolled them for us into sheets of the desired thickness. Quickly, I had some tools and dies made which enabled us to produce as many fish eater blanks as we wished. Not only could we then meet our own requirements but we could also supply fish eater blanks to the trade.

At lunchtimes, when weather permitted, we played football in the yard with other tenants joining in. Amongst these was Basil Walker who, at the time, was manager of the Sheffield Steel Mark Company. Basil has become quite a celebrity in recent years by demonstrating, at the Abbeydale Industrial Hamlet, his incredible skill at producing, entirely by hand and using simple tools, the most intricate steel marks (punches).

Another company, with premises at the bottom of the yard, was Marples & Co., whose only employees were father and son. I believe they continued a business founded by earlier generations. Their workshop was, if anything, more Dickensian than any other I have ever seen. They produced mortise and tenon and other wood gauges, set-squares, spokeshaves and similar joiners' tools. Using mostly rosewood and other hardwoods the quality of their hand-made products was unbelievably good. The mass production techniques introduced by large companies had made Marples' products uncompetitive and they struggled to make a living wage despite their skill and hard work.

The belt-driven equipment they used in their small workshop looked to me like museum pieces even then. Sadly, the demand for their fine quality products was to dry up and, within a short time, they closed down—another chapter of Sheffield's industrial heritage had closed. I believe the son, who was about my own age, only stayed on until his father finally called it a day.

As already stated, the premises were old and decrepit. I was always dashing about between workshops organising production and helping out to relieve bottlenecks wherever they occurred. One day, as I carried a box of knives from the warehouse to the etching room, the floor collapsed! Knives flew in the air as my legs went through the ceiling of the filing shop immediately below. Lath and plaster and clouds of dust rained down on Alice Campbell who quickly made the air bluer still with some of her own inimitable choice phrases. Fortunately, apart from my pride, no one was seriously hurt and very soon howls of laughter erupted from the filing shop when they saw my leg dangling from the ceiling.

A frequent visitor to our works at Arundel Street was Berny Goodman (not to be confused with the well-known Sheffield tailor with a similar name). Berny was a buying agent for a London wholesaler and, during 1950, he was to prove a good friend. I fell ill with appendicitis and, following a routine operation, returned home after seven days but, unknown to the doctors, things had gone horribly wrong—I had a serious internal infection. My bowels ceased to function, pelvic abscesses and adhesions formed and, after a week of agony, I was re-admitted to hospital. I underwent emergency surgery which included the removal of part of my intestines. Streptomycin was administered, night and day, every few hours until I looked and felt like a pin cushion. For several months my life hung in the balance. Because of post-operative pneumonia, the bottom of my back was badly swollen and on one occasion, over a period of several days, my stomach became greatly distended. This proved to be a large internal abscess which eventually burst leaving me lying in puss. I was later told that I was lucky that it burst outwards and not inwards or I would not be here. I still have a large hole alongside my navel which looks like a second belly button.

My troubles were not yet over but, after five months in hospital, I was declared fit enough to be sent to a convalescent home at Grange-over-Sands. However, the internal infection had not cleared up and I again became very ill. The doctor was called in the middle of the night and I was taken by ambulance to Lancaster Royal Infirmary. Although I have no memory of it, the ambulance journey was not without incident as we were involved in an accident en-route. Margaret, my wife of just over a year, who had visited me every day whilst in hospital in Sheffield, had accompanied me to Grange-over-Sands where she stayed at a local guest house.

Purely by coincidence, my dad's brother, Uncle John, who suffered from acute bronchitis having been gassed at Gallipoli during World War I, was also staying at the same convalescent home and he accompanied me to the hospital. When Margaret visited me the next morning, I had tubes passing through my nose into my stomach which were draining blood and puss into a large glass jar at the side of the bed. A saline drip had been inserted into my ankle but had missed the vein, consequently, the solution had been dripping into my leg for several hours causing inflammation. This was being treated with hot kaolin poultices and another drip had been inserted into my arm. Altogether I was in a sorry state. Margaret quickly informed my parents who came to Lancaster immediately. The doctors decided against further surgery, for which I was thankful, and my mother stayed on with Margaret for the two weeks or so that I remained in hospital.

The Lancaster Royal Infirmary was a far cleaner and more efficient hospital than the old Sheffield City General—where more than half of the patients in my ward suffered secondary infections after surgery. One young man in a nearby bed, who was visited every day by his attractive wife and two-year-old daughter, died in the operating theatre after several operations. His last words to me as he was being taken down to the operating theatre for the last time were 'Well Bert, it's shit or bust this time'. I am grateful for the treatment and care I received whilst in Lancaster and consider myself lucky to have been taken there.

On my return to Sheffield I had a consultation with Mr Coxon the surgeon who had performed my emergency operation. He told me nothing further could be done. The internal infection may or may not recur and he advised me to rest. After six months of hospitalisation I'd had all the rest I could cope with and next day I decided to return to work. Berny Goodman had been most helpful during my illness by visiting the factory several times per week, helping with packing and doing whatever he could to assist the warehouse staff. This was an act of kindness for which my family and I were most grateful.

Another customer, a Polish Jew whose name I have, unfortunately, forgotten, was a survivor of the Nazi concentration camps. Every other member of his family had died. He visited me in hospital several times, an unexpected gesture from a comparative stranger. He was a fairly new customer, living in London, who visited Sheffield about once a month buying cutlery and tools. Over the years, through business contacts, I was to make many friends like Mr Goodman and my Polish acquaintance, not only from this country but from many parts of the world. There were, however, a few others I would rather not have met.

Work proved to be the best therapy and, as I regained my strength, I soon became as active as ever, even though the hours were long and the work hard. I thrived on being busy and often felt like a juggler with several balls in the air at the same time. Doing your own thing and being stretched to the limit, both mentally and physically, is enormously stimulating and rewarding as anyone who has experienced that situation for years on end will appreciate. If, like me, you could switch off completely once the day's work was done it does you no harm but it helps to be equally enthusiastic about your leisure activities—and I've always had a whale of a time.

My work was interesting and extremely varied. One minute I could be helping Christine in the office to decipher some complicated export documentation, the next sorting out an argument between Jack and Alice, or being sworn at by buffer lasses complaining about poor quality blanks that were difficult to buff. The next hour or so might find me in the ground-floor back room rushing to pack some goods ready for collection by Tuffnells, the carriers, who called every afternoon. After a quick dash up the stairs to pack smaller parcels for the post, they were then carried down Sycamore Street to the post office at Fitzalan Square for the 5pm deadline. It was then back to work for an hour or more to plan the next day's production and count out the work for the various departments.

This may seem like a one man band but it certainly was not. I preferred my staff to concentrate on manufacturing the goods on order and wanted no hold ups. Production was the most important priority, not only to satisfy customers demands but also to ensure that badly needed cash would come in to enable us to pay our bills and wages. On average it took from 10–12 weeks from the month of despatch before payment was made by customers, a fact often overlooked by some setting up in business, and like most small companies we were under-capitalised, cash flow was a constant problem.

Freddy Webster, the brother of Archie of pedigree maggot fame, was employed to do odd jobs—sweeping, running errands for the employees and generally fetching and carrying. He had been brain damaged at birth and lived with his elderly widowed mother who kept him spotlessly clean and tidy. Whilst she was alive he was well behaved but, after she died, his behaviour sometimes caused problems and his general appearance deteriorated. Most of the time I was able to tolerate his lapses but I sometimes lost my temper and shouted at him—something I often regretted later. Freddy never bore any ill-will and always behaved himself, for a while, after my outbursts.

Our next door neighbours, on the other side of the archway, were an old established firm producing high-quality pen and pocket knives. The name of the company was Wragg & Co. and their ancient trade mark was an Orb and Sceptre. The company was owned by two middle-aged brothers, Sam and Frank Pinchbeck, who lived and worked in London. I believe the business had been in the family for several generations and that they only kept it going out of loyalty to their few, elderly, employees. The fact that the premises were soon to be demolished heralded the end of another Sheffield company.

Pinchbeck Brothers, as they called themselves, were the London agents for several well-known hardware manufacturers who found dealing with an agent more economical than having their own staff and offices in the capital. Sam, the elder brother, came to Sheffield about once a month for discussions with the manager of Wraggs. Shortly after I became manager of our organisation he came to introduce himself and asked whether we had heard anything regarding the impending demolition of the building—we were no wiser than him. I took him round our workshops and warehouse showing him some of our products. Afterwards, back in our office, he asked whether we would be interested in appointing Pinchbeck Brothers as our London Agents. At the time we had no sales staff so, having nothing to lose, I agreed to the appointment for a trial period of one year—they were to remain our agents for the next 25 years. Sam's son, Michael, joined the firm when Sam retired a few years later.

I learned quite a lot from the Pinchbecks. Frank, a graduate from Cambridge University, was extremely thorough, verging on the pedantic. He wrote daily reports concerning the companies he and Sam had visited and, almost invariably, requested samples and quotations for one thing or another. In those days there were many businesses in London known as

Confirming Houses, they acted for overseas groups of stores and wholesale importers in countries throughout the world. Confirming Houses would guarantee payment to the suppliers, this was a great help to small manufacturers like ourselves. They usually paid within a few days of the goods leaving our factory, at the same time taking a discount of 3%.

The Confirming Houses, some of which are now well known Merchant Banks, would periodically see representatives by appointment and, if they saw any products that they thought may interest overseas clients, would ask for samples. Sometimes, the samples would be held in the offices of the Confirming House pending an imminent visit of a buyer from abroad, otherwise, they were airmailed out. All this added greatly to my workload and so I was glad when Bob Price agreed to rejoin the company. This time he stayed until retirement at 65. He became an important part of the team I was building, being responsible for all incoming and outgoing goods, and this, of course, took a great load off me.

Many of the overseas customers for whom the Confirming Houses acted were located in British Commonwealth countries. For every such country special invoice forms, tissue paper thin, were required, often in sextuplicate. The purpose of these Imperial Preference Invoice Forms, which had to be certified and signed by two responsible officials, was to allow British-made goods into the Commonwealth country of destination, either free of duty or at special lower rates. Each country seemed to have slightly different regulations and great care had to be taken to comply with the requirements.

Many overseas buyers coming to the UK would visit the major manufacturing centres, calling on several manufacturers in each location to examine their products. Often in my overalls, having been working on a machine, I would meet these people, several of whom became regular visitors and good friends. There is nothing like personal contact to create confidence between buyer and supplier. With hindsight either I, or someone from our company, should have made regular selling trips to potential overseas countries but there was never time to undertake all the jobs that needed to be done.

Whilst most of the export orders received were comparatively small, averaging £200–£300, occasionally much larger ones were obtained. It was Pinchbeck Brothers who, in the early 1950s, obtained our largest export order to date. This was from The Arabian American Oil Company (Aramco) and was secured after a visit by Sam to their London buying office. The order called for several thousand knives, forks and spoons in Old English pattern stainless steel, each piece to be badged with the company logo (two letter As in a circle). Sheffield-made stainless steel spoons and forks were quite uncommon in the early 1950s, the material was much harder than nickel

'Old English', another traditional design.

silver and required different stamping dies. At the time, the regular blank manufacturers were not interested in producing stainless steel blanks and remained so until forced to change a few years later when the demand for nickel silver ones declined.

One or two of the larger Sheffield cutlery firms had their own blank manufacturing department. Amongst them was Cooper Brothers whose premises, now the Sheffield Science Park, were on Arundel Street not far from our own. Old English pattern was by far the most popular design at the time and was sold in different gauges and qualities; chromium plate, polished nickel silver, EPNS and sterling silver.

Cooper Brothers had the foresight to tool up for this design in medium gauge stainless steel and, having surplus capacity, had offered to supply unfinished blanks to other manufacturers. The works manager, Cyril Whitely, an old friend and, like myself, of the Fellowship of the Services, had told me of this. I ordered a few dozen and, having processed them, sent samples to Pinchbecks. We were therefore quite fortunate to be in the right place with the right product when Aramco were looking for a UK source of supply.

The buffer lasses hated stainless steel which, being much harder than nickel silver, was consequently harder to buff and polish. They told me where I could put them when I took the original prototypes in for processing! There was a great deal of 'effin and blindin' when they learned that I had accepted a large order for stainless steel spoons and forks but, by agreeing generous piecework rates, I was able to mollify their complaints.

Each piece had to be passed by an independent inspectorate before despatch and, afterwards, placed in tin-lined packing cases which had to be soldered in the presence of an inspector. This was another experience in our learning curve which was immediately rewarded by a second order from a subsidiary company of Aramco called Tapline.

'All work and no play makes Jack a dull boy' but we enjoyed plenty of leisure activities. On Saturday afternoons, with sister-in-law Kath, I went to watch Sheffield Wednesday. I enjoyed a few drinks and a sing-along in the Foresters on Division Street, with brother Barry and friends, followed by dancing at the nearby City Hall. Fishing trips to Lincolnshire, Cambridgeshire and North Yorkshire on Sundays, plus an occasional dinner dance and, of course, the work's outings just about completed our recreational pursuits.

Olive Grey, who worked at our St Mary's Road premises, had a grown up family with several of them married On one of our works' outings she caused quite a stir. We had been to Blackpool for the day and on the way home called at a pub in Tintwistle. In front of the pub was a large forecourt with a low wall separating it from the pavement. Elderly local gents used to

Enjoying a weeks' fishing holiday with my brother Barry (on the right) and friends.

sit chatting on the wall on summer evenings until it was time to go inside and have the few drinks they could afford.

It was still quite light when our crowd came out ready to board the bus for the final leg of the journey home. Some of the buffer lasses were singing and generally making merry, which caused the old locals to turn round to see what was going on. Olive, who was turned sixty and quite plump, out of sheer exuberance began to do cartwheels around the forecourt. One old codger, who was enjoying the spectacle of frilly knickers and suspenders being exposed, fell backwards off the wall to cheers and hilarity from the girls.

During the 1950s some of the large Sheffield cutlery companies, spurred on by the modern Scandinavian designs in stainless steel then being imported in small quantities by specialist shops, began to employ internationally known designers for their own products. I believe it was David Mellor, then a young designer, who was commissioned by Walker & Hall to produce a new design for them. He came up with a design which I think was called Peace. Like other modern designs there were only a limited number of items in the range. The cutlery was quite plain with clean, flowing lines, and made from 18-8 stainless steel with a satin finish. As an alternative, in addition to the rather heavy solid monobloc table and dessert knives, these two items were offered with black or white dishwasher-safe, nylon handles. I believe this was one of the best of the post-war cutlery designs. Another designer whose name springs to mind was Robert Welch who, if I remember correctly, designed for Viners.

It was my view that solid stainless steel, or stainless steel combined with modern dishwasher-safe, materials, was where the future of cutlery lay, and I decided to concentrate on these materials for any exclusive designs of our own. Commissioning a professional designer to produce not only drawings but actual prototypes was a costly business and beyond our means at that time. I was not very good at drawing but, given a piece of sheet steel, some steel files and a grindstone, I could develop shapes and contours suitable for cutlery design. For the handles I could do the same with blocks of Xylonite and so my next exclusive design, 'Nycraft' evolved. Nycraft combined mirror-polished stainless steel with black, dishwasher-safe, nylon handles. The design was quite functional and, when submitted to the newly created Council of Industry Design, was accepted by them for inclusion in their Design Index. This index was a huge directory containing photographs and specifications of well-designed, British made products. Design Index was consulted by architects and the like, responsible for equipping and furnishing buildings and, for a small annual fee, you could display the actual products at the Design Index premises in the Haymarket, London.

'Nycraft', the second exclusive range of cutlery I designed.

It was to here that Lady Hamilton, chairperson of an organisation which, I think, was called The Rheumatism and Arthritis Foundation of the United Kingdom, went in search for products suitable for use by people with impaired holding ability. Although Nycraft had been designed to be light and functional, its use by people who could not pick up or hold conventional cutlery had not been envisaged. Her Ladyship telephoned, personally, and asked me to send some samples to the Nuffield Orthopaedics Hospital in Oxford, they tested it with their patients and found it suitable.

Towards the end of 1954 the Sheffield City Council wrote to all the tenants of the Arundel Street factory informing them of its impending demolition. The Council had purchased a large factory in Matilda Street, formerly the property of Deakins (Silversmiths) Limited. It was being split up into various workshops and each tenant was invited to have a look round with a view to leasing part of the property.

I obtained the key and, with Barry and my father, had a good look round. Being the first company to show an interest in renting space we could choose whatever workshops we wanted. We chose the ground floor front for the warehouse and the central floor workshop, formerly a plating shop, for our grinding and glazing department. Foolishly, we chose the fourth and fifth floor

'Finecraft', the third pattern I designed. Many hundreds of thousands of pieces of Finecraft were supplied to Berni Inns.

for our cutlers, polishing and buffing shops. Foolish because, although there was good light up there, for years afterwards heavy boxes of cutlery had to be carried up and down the flights of stairs for processing. The elderly buffers and polishers complained constantly of 'Them bloody stairs'.

The move from our Arundel Street and St Mary's Road workshops to 111 Matilda Street which, for the first time during my managership, brought all our operations under one roof, seems an appropriate place to end this, the first part of my recollections of the post-war Sheffield cutlery industry to a close. I hope to continue the story at some later date.

A multi-polishing machine for cutlery production developed and built by H. Housley (Engineers) Limited.